WHERE WAS GOD LAST FRIDAY?

Where Was God Last Friday?

Geoffrey Crees

Hodder & Stoughton
LONDON SYDNEY AUCKLAND

First published in Great Britain 1995

British Library Cataloguing in Publication Data
A record for this book is available from the British Library

ISBN 0 340 63048 5

Typeset by Hewer Text Composition Services, Edinburgh
Printed and bound in Great Britain by
Cox & Wyman Ltd, Reading, Berkshire

Hodder and Stoughton
A division of Hodder Headline PLC
338 Euston Road
London NW1 3BH

Dedicated
in thanksgiving to God
for
Sheree, Ian, Paula, Paul, and Lindy,
to
their parents and families

Contents

Illustrations

Acknowledgements

The writing and production of this book have been made possible only through the kindness, generosity and time of a number of people.

Among them are Peter Sandall, Press/Public Relations Officer for Wiltshire Constabulary; Jim Akers; Christine Parkyn, Headteacher Moredon Junior School; Susan Pagett, Deputy Headteacher Moredon Infants School; various friends who offered and gave hospitality, and especially to Tony and Audrey Pinkney of Priscilla Trust, who made available their delightful cottage in France where much of the original work was written.

Special gratitude is due to Alister Redfern, Director of In-Service Training in Bristol Diocese, and to a long-time friend Gordon Oliver, Director of Training in Rochester Diocese, both of whom helpfully scrutinised the text, and whose comments were searching and relevant.

Significant, too, are the welcome contributions made by Clive Okill (now teaching in North Devon); John Spanton, Nurse Therapist at Marlborough Children's Hospital; Barbara Richards, Senior Chaplain at Princess Margaret Hospital, Swindon; and not least to Dr Claire Lapthorn, Consultant Psychiatrist at Roundway Hospital, Devizes, for assistance with Chapter 6.

A considerable amount of the original script was drafted as a project during study leave and therefore I am grateful for the financial assistance received at that time from the Diocese of Bristol Sarum, St Michael's Trust and St Mary's District Church Council, Rodbourne Cheney. My thanks also need to be recorded to Raymond Adams and Meg Guillebaud who, during my sabbatical leave, took on an increased work load in what is already a busy and demanding parish.

My sabbatical leave after twenty-five years in the ordained ministry was originally envisaged as a period of thirteen weeks; it then became ten weeks and, because of my involvement with the families at the trial at Gloucester Crown Court became, in the end, only eight weeks! Any lack of finesse, however, is my own responsibility, not through lack of time.

Gratitude must be expressed for the assistance to a novice author from Eric Major of Hodder Headline whose perusal of the original text saw the possibility of wider publication.

I am also indebted to John Gladwin, whom I have known since Durham college days, for sparing the time to write such a gentle and generous Foreword.

My thanks are also due to Pat Brett who typed some of the text, to Angela Lyne who coped with a good deal of the necessary correspondence and last, and by no means least, to Jean, my wife, who deciphered my scribble, typed the script and made many a helpful and pertinent comment and without whose help very little would have been accomplished.

Foreword

The importance and significance of the day-to-day pastoral and teaching ministry of the Church become very evident at moments of personal and community crisis. When the Hillsborough football disaster hit both Sheffield and Liverpool, people flooded into open churches. Thousands poured into Sheffield Cathedral. That experience in the Church is replicated whenever people face a personal crisis. Frequently they want to pray, to have time for tears and for quiet reflection, and they need the help of people skilled in pastoral care.

People have to be set aside for such sensitive and important work. Such people will be trained both through reflection of their own personal experience and through developing specific caring skills. One of the strong themes running through this book is the need for such people and for such training. The priest who gets stopped on the street and asked for help or who enters a home and discovers levels of distress not evident from outside needs such skills. Especially is this so in communities suffering the aftermath of disaster.

In reading this book you will become aware of the wonder of God's purpose. Geoffrey Crees is the parish priest of St Mary's Church, Rodbourne Cheney, in Swindon. On Friday 13 September 1991, a car, out of control, crashes into a bench on which a number of children were sitting at the side of the road, five die and two others are seriously injured. Suddenly a community is thrown into trauma. The mystery of God's purpose is revealed in the very special skills possessed by Geoffrey Crees. His own life story, revealed so sensitively here, gave him both the experience and the training to be a pivotal person in helping both the families and the community cope with and come through this terrible accident.

Our understanding and experience of God, in a deep and often inexplicable way, grows out of such awfulness. In reading this book we are made to think again about our faith, to consider how well we prepare people for the realities of pastoral ministry and to work on any experience we have had of people and communities living in grief.

In a country which, in recent years, has suffered Bradford and Hillsborough football tragedies, the Lockerbie Jumbo Jet disaster, the sinking of the *Herald of Free Enterprise*, the Kings Cross Tube fire, the Hungerford shootings and this dreadful accident in Swindon, we need the help of this book. Above all we need to grow in our understanding of the One who shares our griefs and carries our sorrows.

John Gladwin, Bishop of Guildford
formerly Provost of Sheffield Cathedral

Introduction

This book is an attempt to give some provisional answers to the
question posed by its title and to show lessons learned when
one is pitched, quite unexpectedly, into a crisis situation. The
question was initially asked by the preacher, my colleague,
at the first funeral service following the horrendous Akers
Way road accident in September 1991. This question was
taken up and distorted by the local press and an apology was
later given.

Nevertheless, the question remains.

It is an easy cliché to say we live in a world of disasters, but increasing media attention has, in recent years,
brought the horrors of Lockerbie, Hillsborough, Zeebrugge,
and the loss of the *Estonia* in the Baltic, among others,
into the homes of billions of people who otherwise might
only have been aware of such events in a marginal way.
The list seems like the roll of battle honours on regimental
colours.

However, although the 'disaster scenario' has become more
immediate and real to people now than in previous generations, ever since man has been on this earth conflict,
pain, cruelty, starvation, famine, war, crime and accident
have been very much part of human life. It has often been
observed that it is the western world's general attitude to
death itself that makes many people ill-prepared for its sudden
happening and unable to cope when it occurs on a larger
scale. Michael Ramsey in *The Christian Priest Today* wrote,
'A country, town or village may feel itself to be peaceful
and secure but upheavals of one kind or another can be
very near.'[1]

Wars! Disasters! Accidents! Tragedy continues to be the experience of humankind. The consequences and the repercussions live on in the minds of those affected. Christians cannot ignore such events. Careful reflection can, and should, bring new spiritual insights. The following is just one contribution to the debate that will last until the Second Coming itself brings the travails of this world to a close.

Jesus spoke of 'wars and rumours of wars' (Matt. 24:6). His followers were told to expect tribulation and He castigated those who promised false peace.

To put disasters into categories for instance might be easy, seemingly natural ones like earthquakes or volcanic eruptions; devised ones such as Joseph Stalin's purges in the 1930s, or Hitler's Holocaust or the wars which never cease; or the tragic ones of air, road, rail and sea; or disasters in embryonic form such as the effect of acid rain or the loss of the ozone layer. Putting suffering in various categories may be useful but it goes only some way in explaining why a loving God should allow such events to happen. Whether one person or millions are involved, the pain and trauma are just as intense for those caught up in such tragedies.

The immediate raison d'être for this book was the accident on Friday 13 September 1991, on Akers Way, Swindon, Wiltshire, in which five young people were killed and two very seriously injured, and my pastoral involvement with the families ever since. On 30 September 1992, at Gloucester Crown Court, one driver involved was found guilty of causing death by reckless driving and sentenced to five years' imprisonment. The jury found the driver of another car involved not guilty of the same charge but guilty of careless driving.

This was a disaster, not on the horrific scale of a Bangladeshi flood or the Japanese earthquake of 1995, but something that was very local. (The convicted driver had attended the same school as those killed, and his parents live only a minute's walk away from some of the families involved.) So locality as well as scale has a great deal to do with our understanding of disaster and its effects.

In this instance, as will be seen later, although the event did reach the national headlines there was an acute feeling of 'Why did it happen here?' and 'Why us of all people?' The sheer innocence of the victims would also enhance the idea that 'nothing is real unless it is local'.

For the Christian, no understanding of disasters, whether large or small, international, national or local, can be divorced from the cross of Christ, which can be seen as a man-made 'disaster', but through which the salvation of the world can be realised and discovered.

Indeed, it might be argued that, if the churches' response to disaster is often seen as marginal or inadequate, it is not because Christians have nothing to contribute in such situations, or are afraid of interfering, but because our theological perception is inadequate.

George Carey, the present Archbishop of Canterbury, has written about 'a shift of focus from a Trinitarian faith, anchored in the centrality of Christ, to a vague amorphous belief in God in which Christ is not the definitive focus . . . resulting in stunted Christians, but also in a pitiful reductionist Church life'.[2]

One of the compelling reasons behind this book is to enquire what would happen if disaster, whether great or small, landed at the doorstep of our local church? How would that church – its membership and its leaders – respond?

1

Here I Am

Of all the chapters in this book I have found this one the hardest to write! This is not because I don't know the subject, and I trust it is not out of any false modesty, but a book which is at heart about other people, and especially their grief and loss and attempts to explore engagement with a living God should not, in my judgement, include too much detail about the all-too-human author. Yet, for all this, the reader is at obvious disadvantage if the writer hides behind a cloak of anonymity as if an 'invisible hand' has penned the pages.

I love libraries! To me they are like an Aladdin's cave full of great treasures. The writer of Ecclesiastes says 'of making many books there is no end' (12:12). Despite that there are areas in our local library which I rarely use. The first is the autobiography section, the second is the sci-fi. I avoid the one because such books often seem to be published to promote an 'image' or for the purpose of self-aggrandisement, the second because I am simply not interested in the subject, however popular it may be. Nevertheless, everyone has their own story to tell.

In 'telling my story', some of which will not be very original, it is my hope it will be of use to others in the future. In one sense there can never be adequate preparation for disasters and their sudden happening, but the emergence of major disaster plans in the UK and, indeed, the sophistication and speed of response of emergency services in crisis situations obviously needs continual fine tuning. The role of clergy in such situations has been clearly defined and even in post-Christian society is still very welcome whether, say, in the giving of last rites or in after care. Our society is not so secular as to dismiss the spiritual needs of the victim and the carer. The fact that the accident, which will be examined in considerable depth in later pages, occurred some 600 yards from the local (and very visible) Anglican church and that four of the funerals took place within its walls, make it hard to divorce Christian activity from its role in the community. The great glory of the Church of England has been in the past its system of pastoral care; it is an arrangement not without its critics but, when something of national interest occurs locally, it is often the rector or vicar who has to respond and on whom the attention of the media is focused.

My only justification for writing as I have done is not because I have any great claims in the world of moral or pastoral theology but simply to claim that God has taught me a great deal from one particular tragic event and from that there may be experiences to be shared with others. Indeed it could and should be a 'learning experience' for the whole Church but it is those privileged to be 'up front' in such situations who have the most to reflect upon.

Put another way, there does need to be the best possible pastoral care available and provided when an event such as a disaster occurs, whatever its scale, for both those affected and those who care, but also implementation of truths discovered and, for the Christian leader(s) some theological reflection as a continuing part of Christian growth.

St Paul, who knew a good deal about crisis management, put it this way 'I have learnt to be satisfied with what I have. I know what it is to be in need and what it is to have more than enough. I have learnt this secret so that anywhere, at any time, I am content whether I am full or hungry, whether I have too much or too little. I have the strength to face all conditions by the power that Christ gives me' (Phil. 4:11b–13). Elsewhere he wrote 'Who then, can separate us from the love of Christ? Can trouble do it, or hardship or persecution or hunger or poverty or danger or death? . . . No, in all these things we have complete victory through him who loved us! For I am certain that nothing can separate us from his love' (Rom. 8:35 37–38a).

The one abiding memory I have of my brief sojourn at theological college in the lovely cathedral city of Durham, was the dictat never to apologise in public. Standing in front of an audience or congregation and attempting to make explanations would immediately set the speaker at a psychological disadvantage with the hearers. It is a rule I have broken more than once! If it is true with public speaking it is also a fact when it comes to writing something of substance for public consumption. Most clergy though often aspiring to write something substantial never get beyond the 300–400 words necessary for their monthly contribution to the parish magazine. My aim is something more than that: a desire to open up a subject on which much ink has been used already but to relate it to one particular event and the way it has affected and still does affect a large number of people. The substantial list of people whose support I have drawn upon will show that, although I have been identified as the author, much credit goes elsewhere.

How then can such a book be justified? Why add one more volume to the accounts of disasters on library shelves? Will it not open up wounds which, although they can never be completely removed are, at least, beginning to heal a little. I think I need to state that I am deeply conscious of that aspect. I do not want the charge of hypocrisy to be laid against me or to open what essentially was, and still is, private grief, into further public discussion. Nevertheless, I trust this book will achieve in a modest way a number of things.

Foremost is a renewal of faith in the living Christ who died and rose again for the whole of humankind. It is out of that faith I write not out of some voyeuristic motive.

Second, as a help to those who believe in Jesus and still ask great questions, and who find it hard to answer the doubters and atheists when they, in turn, ask such questions.

Third, to communicate some understanding of God's love to those outside the Christian faith who, in my judgement, and indeed the Biblical stance, are missing out on so much in this life and, more especially, in the life to come.

Fourth, as an aid to theological students as they prepare for the great calling of Christian service and if possible to make them aware of what may be demanded of them should they ever face such a situation.

Here then, I hope, is something for the committed Christian, those on the edge of God's family and those in both groups, who live and work in and around the town of Swindon and beyond. All tragedies are, in a sense, local and many of them acquire a title which relates to a particular place, others the cause of the tragedy. Some, like the Titanic sinking acquire a mystic quality and folklore which, in the course of time, tends to blur the scale of the disaster.

If Christians involved in a crisis situation are not eventually drawn closer to the Lord Jesus and are unable to draw others to Him then no matter how expert they are in such situations they will have failed the One he or she claims to represent and serve. But, having said that, it does also need to be recognised that some Christians are not drawn closer to their Lord in such situations. The reasons for this may well lie elsewhere though I suspect it is more likely to be a matter of spiritual immaturity than anything else.

This book, then, is not the story of an accident or the verbatim accounts of some of the people involved, as such would have needed to be more contemporaneous with the event itself. Yet, without reflective thought on such human drama many more questions will remain unanswered. Out of sensitivity to the bereaved and injured families I have kept details of the horror to the minimum possible. I am aware, however, that publication will reawaken some memories and pain but, I believe, in God's time and His healing plan, greater good will come out of this having been written.

On a far more objective level, an event such as this is a part of the chronicles of a town and its people. I have attempted to be both objective in cataloguing the events of an evening in Swindon in September 1991, and also subjective in sharing some of my own personal history. The fact that it is being written a considerable time after the event itself does, I hope, show little desire to rush into print which, in my view, is an all-too-common habit these days.

My intention was to produce a mature reflection on an event in which one was both involved and not involved at the same time; involved in the sense of being pastor to people whose hearts ache for seemingly unnecessary deaths; not involved in the sense that they were not my own children or even friends', but parishioners'. I have always treated my relationship with parishioners as that of potential friends, a much closer one than, say, that of a doctor and patient, or a Member of Parliament and constituent. It is both intimate and distant at the same time.

Sangster, the great Methodist preacher of several decades ago said 'There is nothing worse than wasted suffering, to go through the pain and achieve nothing from it is indeed a waste'. It is my hope that this writing will, in some sense, minimise the seeming waste of life on that September evening and indeed, bring further glory to the One who created us and designed us for Himself.

Unlike the ancient Ermine Street, which for centuries provided something of a western boundary to Swindon, Akers Way is a modern road built in the 1950s. Swindon, in common with many towns, is in the habit of naming roads after prominent sons and daughters, witness Wildern Square and Fleming Way to give two examples.

Francis Akers farmed land to the west of St Mary's Church in Rodbourne Cheney. He became Mayor of Swindon and so, when a new road was needed to service three new schools, a housing estate and an industrial complex, the decision was made to name the new highway after someone who had given much to the area in the town. He is now buried along with his wife in St Mary's churchyard within sight and sound of the road he, in part, helped to create. Of the farm, little or nothing remains, but the road named after him is now sadly, not the reminder it was of a loyal citizen but the painful one of a September night of tragedy.

I make no apologies that this book lacks what is essential in the Christian character, a sense of fun and laughter. If it is missing it is because it disappeared in the needless deaths of five young people. It takes a long while for the smile to return in the face of such personal tragedy.

The year of George V's Silver Jubilee when storm clouds were gathering in Nazi Germany was also the time when I entered this world. How my parents afforded a nursing home for my mother's confinement I shall never know but, although the building opposite what is now Brunel University in Uxbridge still exists, its function has long been changed.

My father was a bank clerk who had been moved to a new branch of his bank from the city and had subsequently met my mother after the move. I was to be their only child. We were not a particularly religious family though we did have some good biblical names to boast of, as my paternal grandmother who died when I was seven was Peninnah and the name Jesse occurs several times in recent lineage. How my parents met I never learned.

The atmosphere in the road where I spent twenty-seven years of my life was a happy one and it provided a secure environment. Of the forty-five houses surrounded by 'green belt' I can still name the occupants of that period, especially three of them! We lived at number 21, my maternal grandmother, aunt, uncle and two cousins at number 17, and my paternal grandparents at number 13. There were several other single-children families and we spent much of our free time together. Sheila who lived next door was eleven days younger than I and the nearest I had to a sister.

The intervention of the war was, of course, a dramatic event in our formative years. In 1940 my father was called up, eventually to be commissioned in the Pay Corps. Holidays now took on a new dimension as my mother and I spent some of the school holidays in the Isle of Man and Leeds, where my father had been posted. For all that, the horrors of war did not really touch me. Yes, there were lessons in the air raid shelter in the local village school. Yes, there were bombs in the park opposite and at the end of our street, and we did have soot down our chimney when 'doodle-bugs' landed a mile away, yet somehow the reality escaped me. I had known very little of peace so this was normal life!

However, as I grew older the war came to an end and, of course, my memories become clearer – not least the events of VE and VJ Days. The joy of the latter was clouded by being 'lost' after I became separated from my mother outside Buckingham Palace where we had gone to join the celebrations.

So childhood was a real mixture of the somewhat idyllic surroundings of rural life with easy access to London, 'helping' in Granny's shop, watching the boats on the canal, playing and swimming in the adjacent and as yet unpolluted rivers and local gravel-pit, helping the local farmer at haymaking time and learning to milk a cow by hand. What more could a young boy wish for?

The war years affected us all. My uncle was taken prisoner in Crete, my father was absent for long periods, proximity to London meant we were never far away from hostilities. Where was God? I cannot even remember thinking about Him. We knew the church in the village, we knew the vicar and the embarrassment when the curate called on us unexpectedly!

Any real Christian engagement was still far in the future. After a fractured education, partly due to the war and partly to a continuous succession of childhood illnesses, I eventually left school. I was not academic and really did not know what to do. By some minor miracle I had passed the 13+ exam and had attended Slough Technical School. It seemed logical therefore that I should follow some form of engineering apprenticeship. It was not really what I wanted to do but it was better than the bank for which my father was pressing! In truth, without any career guidance I had no idea of what I wanted by way of a job or what I desired from life. My school leaving certificate with five passes was rejected as valueless by most employers and so I had, in the end, to rely on my father's influence via the bank to secure an apprenticeship.

Work began at 7.30 a.m. for £2 a week. For the most part I found it tedious and tiring, but I was granted day-release to study for an ONC in electrical engineering. This had two effects: first it delayed National Service and second it meant a day a week away from the factory. Scouting and sport were not only my hobbies but also my 'gods'. I had attempted the first level of HNC twice and had failed, although I had told friends I had passed; but the requirements of Her Majesty prevailed and eventually I found myself being called up for National Service. Although my background in Scouting was useful this was the biggest change in young adulthood.

Blandford, Honiton, Arborfield and eventually Cyprus became familiar to me. Two attempts to gain officer training both failed, ironically it seems mostly due to my lack of ability to give a simple five-minute talk!

'Mum, I've been posted to Cyprus!'

Whether these words were a shock to my parents, to me or my newly acquired girlfriend I have no means of recalling, but

they did make a real 'sea change' in life. Before long Craftsman
Crees was packed into a DC6 of Eagle Airways for a cramped
six-and-a-half hour flight to the Med.

After I got out of the aircraft one of the first sights was a
shepherd leading his flock of sheep and goats across the edge
of the runway. The biblical significance of that picture certainly
did not register with any of us. Now it is a favourite sermon
illustration!

Where was God in all this?

I had no real sense of God's presence. The local church (in
Iver) was not foreign ground to me. I had been baptised and
also confirmed there, the latter mainly to placate the wishes of
my parents. The vicar even came to see me in the local hospital
when I had had a minor operation. I was the only patient in
the ward at the time and did not know 'the dodge' of either
pretending 'to be asleep or dead' when the parson calls!

Nevertheless the Christian fellowship at Arborfield where I
spent a year training and the evidence of Christ in some of
the people there eventually had a sort of spiritual influence
on me.

One or two of us decided to go to church in Nicosia seven
miles from our camp. On leaving the base we were taunted
as to whether we were 'going for a jump'. My negative reply
stemmed more from my moral middle-class upbringing than
Christian conviction.

After demob it was back to work in the drawing office to
which dizzy heights I had risen after my so-called apprenticeship. Yet the unseen hand of God was at work in my life for, in
the last year of National Service, Christ had become real to me. It
had not been a 'Damascus road' experience but a series of small
trigger points: a visit to the Holy Land (from Cyprus); someone
sent me a book called *Basic Christianity* which gathered more
dust than it was actually read but it had some effect, and not
least the prayers of those who saw my need of Jesus. So although
I was back home to my old job, to Scouting and sport, somehow
I was a changed person. Church membership and worship now
took on a new meaning.

For all that I was twenty-four, still somewhat shy and

lacking in confidence, and it was no wonder relationships with the opposite sex were somewhat tenuous and short-lived. However, within the church there were two new members, both schoolteachers and named Jenny. Within eighteen months both girls had married members of the church and I was one of them!

After two years' home from the army another stirring was going on in my heart. My fiancée had said, 'Have you ever thought about the ministry?' We were now involved in running Pathfinders, a mixed Bible class for young teenagers. The thought had never really occurred to me, but discussions with my vicar led to a provisional selection though I had to obtain two 'O'-levels before full acceptance.

On getting married I reluctantly gave up Scouting in which I had been involved for twenty years. It was big wrench but deep down I felt God calling me to other forms of service. We settled down to married life at the other end of the village, two miles away from my parents' home, young, naïve, but very much in love.

Eventually I secured a place at Cranmer Hall, Durham, to train for ordination. My colleagues in the drawing office where I worked (not the one of my apprenticeship) were puzzled in the extreme but I left with their warm interest and good wishes.

Durham was different!

Here was a shock to the system. This academy was a far cry from the drawing office. It took time to settle down; I barely lasted the first term but somehow through God's grace I survived. It was fine for those who had been through university life and had now progressed to theological college but for me this was very different.

Eventually I began to enjoy it and not least to make some very good friends. We lived outside Durham in a new house which was half the price of the one we sold in Iver. Jenny obtained a post in an infant school in a nearby mining village and soon an amicable system of school, study and training evolved. My old firm was willing to employ me during vacations so that financially at least we more than made ends meet.

Dark clouds, however, were gathering over Jenny's health.

Whether it was related to our desperate desire for a family I cannot now say. She had given up teaching after my first year in college and had actually started studying with six other women. This innovation in college life was not without its repercussions, but she enjoyed the challenge while at the same time finding that she needed more and more psychiatric care for depression.

The clouds lifted for quite some time though as my first curacy (at Hoddesdon) approached. There had been four previous fruitless visits to other parishes, including one where we had to 'baby-sit' whilst the vicar and his wife went out for the evening and I developed flu on the way back to Durham!

On a glorious late-summer day I was ordained in St Alban's Abbey. It was a day never to be forgotten, almost like getting married. Friends and family were there, the service was inspiring and there was so much to look forward to by way of serving the Lord. This was it! Looking back on that day I can truthfully say, despite many heartaches personally and many disappointments, I regret not one day of my ordained ministry.

Life after ordination was demanding and enjoyable. This was where we both felt called to serve. Certainly, although I was thirty-two, I was very inexperienced. I had never been to a funeral let alone seen a dead body.

On a personal level we continued enquiries and tests regarding lack of fertility. With Jenny's depression having lifted, a rich and rewarding time ensued, but towards the end of our time in Hoddesdon Jenny's mother, was diagnosed as having a malignant brain tumour. It was terrible news. Marion had not been a Christian very long; she was fifty-six and had supplied the drive and imagination to the whole of her family.

Following her distressing illness and painful death it was not surprising that a reaction built up in Jenny's mind. She made a serious attempt on her life. By now we had moved to a second curacy at Harwell and Chilton in Oxfordshire, and I found myself on a hectic drive across London to the intensive care unit of the Brook Hospital at Woolwich.

By prompt action on her brother's part – Jenny having been at her parents' home – and good medical care, she recovered and, as far a I know, the parish knew little about it. We moved house to the smaller of the two villages and then the opportunity came to go back to Durham for a study week. It was June – high summer. I teamed up with some other ex-students of Cranmer Hall to journey together.

Jenny's dead

Gently, very gently, Bruce broke the news to me. I could not take it in. Repeated phone calls home had produced no reply and I was indeed becoming very concerned. Bruce had taken the call, told the staff and then, as a good friend should, put it in the most palatable way he could. Then came the wearisome journey home. A difficult inquest and painful, yet triumphant funeral were to follow. She was thirty-three and in many ways had so much to live for. Where were you, God? I lay on the bed and wept bitterly.

Life on my own seemed strange. Church members were kindness itself. I rarely had a Sunday lunch at home and was frequently invited out to other meals. Many were as puzzled and perplexed as I felt deep within myself. The first funeral I officiated at after my own loss was indeed difficult. Friends outside the parish helped. My attempts at explanation were often clumsy and confused.

Good friends included me in their holiday. It was an enjoyable time but I was to make up a foursome; the only difficulty arose on the ferry journey to Ostend when an acquaintance, who also happened to be travelling, asked if this was my new girlfriend. Bereaved clergy can suffer double isolation both from the loss of the person and that which is often part of such a post anyway.

My parents wanted to take me back under their wing but I was able to resist such open pressures. Three weeks after Jenny's death her other brother was married. The twin feelings of joy and sorrow were, I guess, most acute at that point.

There were all the usual things to attend to when a relative dies: executing the will, disposing of possessions. One poignant moment was the occasion when I visited a neighbour farmer's wife. Several weeks earlier she had offered to take Jenny's clothes to a charity shop in Didcot. She had duly sorted and bundled them up and, as I thought, disposed of them. Now, in her lounge, there they still were! Sometimes very little incidents like that, albeit I guess a temporary lapse on the part of a kind helper, can cause such pain.

However, life and ministry had to go on. Living in a small village obviously meant that many people knew about my situation. Most, even if they were not church members, were very kind. There was plenty to do, and the lively youth group did much to keep me on a level path. Other people's needs were much greater than my own, and playing cricket or walking the dog on the downs kept me fit.

It was a time of readjustment. I enjoyed the company of friends well outside the parishes I had been involved in and I had Jesus as Lord, Friend and Saviour. I had His work to do and I had no real notion of loneliness as such, but the sense of loss and the shock of being single again were still very acute. I can well understand how people in such situations look for some sort of quick compensation and then often live to regret such hasty decisions of the heart.

Shopping has never had a great attraction for me but it was a great trial to have to shop for one. I remember I even experimented for a couple of weeks to see how little I could live on. It was amazing to realise how much was normally spent on housekeeping. Adjustment also includes making a fair number of mistakes but the Lord kept me from making too many social errors. They were harder to take from other people in their adjustment to me. Someone who knew how and when Jenny had died inadvertently asked months later how she was getting on at her college course!

In all the personal trauma I saw little of the press and did not hear the local radio. Sometime later someone did show me what the local paper had printed, and I am glad to say it was very restrained and kept to the facts. Were the tragedy to have happened some twenty years later it would have made a much different story. Times have changed in just two decades as my comments in the chapter dealing with the media will bear out. It was now eight months since Jenny had died. I had served my time in two curacies and I had been in the ordained ministry over four-and-a-half years.

A new ministry

What did my future hold? I have never been very career minded, even less so since ordination. I had served two very contrasting curacies, one in suburbia and the other in a more rural setting. At thirty-six I was ready for a move to an incumbent post. A member of the diocesan patronage board did make an informal approach about a parish which meant moving only a couple of miles, but having taken early morning services there I knew it was not the place for me.

I have never seen posts in the ordained ministry as 'jobs' and, if the Anglican ministry lacks a real career structure, it is not necessarily because of its historical roots or the incredible security which until now has been part of its ethos.

However, within twelve months of Jenny's death the then Bishop of Reading wrote offering the living at Greenham some fourteen miles away. Situated on the edge of Newbury, it was (and is) in many ways an ideal parish. It had a variety of housing, a racecourse, industry, farms and, of course, Greenham Common airbase. The real problem of the church was not that fabric repairs were pressing, in fact they were not over-excessive, but that the congregation was minute due partly, in my judgment, to the previous ministry – or lack of it. The one meeting I had with my predecessor was while looking over the rambling vicarage. From comments he made I gathered he did not look too favourably on those 'over him in the Lord'. Suffice it to say there had been spiritualist involvement in both the worship and the vicar's attendance at such meetings elsewhere. He died in hospital of a mysterious illness while, at the same time, his wife had for several months been living with the then churchwarden.

The bizarre situation which I inherited would lend itself to the pages of another book. For all that, a few godly people had clung on tenaciously in their worship and they, along with others, proved to be the essential support in those early, yet heady days when I had to get used to being called 'vicar'. So still in a sense of bereavement I started out on what was a

demanding task. I did not feel lonely: my parents tried to see
to that! I experienced an emptiness inside which, in spite of my
now disciplined prayer life, was hard to fill.

'What time are the services?'

The telephone rang early in the new year, and the female
caller said she and her daughter wanted to come to worship on
Sunday and would like to know details. People were actually
now coming to the church where I was vicar! Something was
happening. Something was happening indeed!

I looked round the tiny congregation, but the mother and
her daughter had not appeared, so the next day I diligently
visited the enquirers. They lived about two miles away outside
the parish. Jean was a widow whose husband had died of a heart
attack following a long illness.

The meeting was not unimportant as within three weeks we
were planning to be married. We kept our secret until Easter and
then announced it in the local paper and awaited the response.
All the counsel I offered to others to be cautious in affairs
of the heart went out of the window! Suddenly I had acquired
an instant family with two young teenagers. Life was not going
to be the same again. Nevertheless Jean and I knew in our heart
of hearts God had called us to serve Him together.

'It's a big job'

After nine years at Greenham (eight of them together) and after
pushing at various doors we found ourselves in East Hull. It was
as different from Greenham as one could imagine. I was leader
of a team of four clergy in a parish of 37,000 people. As the
Bishop said at our initial meeting, 'It's a big job, Geoffrey.'
Whether this meant big in opportunities or the task itself I was
not sure.

It was hard but rewarding. Four tiny churches in a sea of
'unchurched' people. Originally we were dubious about moving
northwards but my godly second vicar Eric said simply, 'Think
of the need, Geoffrey, think of the need'. Within six months I
also found myself as Area Dean of East Hull.

Other storm clouds were gathering, however, in the shape of my parents' health which began to deteriorate. We had felt quite happy leaving them in their small bungalow in Dorset. They were very active in the years after my father retired. Now four years after we moved to Hull each was in a different hospital at the same time.

My Mother's death was broken to me as I rang the hospital having just returned to Hull. Our car knew the route from Hull almost better than we did.

Sometime following my mother's death a notice in the church press caught my eye. Were we being called to move again? East Hull was a great place to work for God but there were other demands. In 1988 we moved to Swindon, I as team rector of Rodbourne Cheney.

Wouldn't it be nice if the family were waiting for us?

This casual remark as we sailed into Poole Harbour on our return from a holiday was soon dismissed as it was Thursday and they would be working. The ferry nudged into dock, we landed and the sun continued to shine as it had done for the previous two weeks, and to our amazement, as we came round the corner of the customs shed, we were greeted by friendly waving arms. They had come after all. 'Let's go to Upton Park for a cup of tea,' they suggested.

The purpose of the short trip up the road and the comforting cup of tea soon become clear. My father had died suddenly the previous Sunday. He had walked the 300 yards to the cricket ground from the nursing home where he had lived. He was a non-playing member of the club, an avid watcher of the game he loved. Membership entitled him to tea at the ground. Tragically he choked while eating a sandwich and all efforts to revive him failed. He was pronounced dead on arrival at the same hospital where my mother had died.

The day after our return we had to attend the inquest, which was not the easiest of homecomings. He was elderly, one month short of his eighty-fifth birthday but it was still painful. How difficult it is to live with the truth that 'in the midst of life we are in death' (Book of Common Prayer funeral service).

Were all the sudden deaths in my family, as well as those of Jean's parents, a preparation for future ministry? Maybe, but I became aware of a lack in my ministerial training in that little time was spent in preparing individuals to minister to their own family and almost no guidance given to help individuals face such a crisis in their own lives. If this is true for ordained men and women, it is more so for their spouses.

The situation may well have changed but there is often the expectation from congregations and others that the minister is impervious to such strains or might indeed never have to encounter them. It is not a question of wearing one's heart on one's sleeve but about honesty and human need.

Who indeed pastors the pastors?

So there have been at least five sudden deaths in my own family, two of them involving inquests and post mortems, and in addition I have conducted countless funerals. In some small way, these were all a preparation for the events of Friday, 13 September 1991.

Coping with personal pain can be an example to others. Neither hiding nor parading it is a delicate balance, but essentially it is about following the One who knew what real suffering was about. As the prophet Isaiah puts it, 'he endured the suffering that should have been ours, the pain we should have borne' (53:4 GNB).

I have attempted to show how human the writer is or, as the letter to the Hebrews puts it in describing Jesus, 'We do not have a high priest who is unable to sympathise with our weaknesses' (Heb. 4:15). The ability to empathise with weakness is surely one of the hallmarks of effective Christianity.

But no pastor, least of all an Anglican one, committed as he or she is to a wide spectrum of ministry, can afford to ignore local feelings, social classes, or the character which is epitomised by the word 'place'. We may live in a 'global village' but a sense of belonging, or fitting in, is all part of what it means to be human.

To this end, some sense of 'local theology' is vital and woe betide the minister who is unaware of this or ignores it. He or she may well want to challenge such local beliefs prophetically, may counsel people away from unChristlike myths, but to ignore their existence can lead to a ministry which is isolated from the world and, therefore, only useful within a very tight-knit circle.

2

Swindon's Local Theology and History

Local Theology

What do we mean by 'local theology'? Put simply, it concerns the beliefs (and practices) which though perhaps not Christocentric appertain to certain places and not others. It may vary from, say, beliefs about Stonehenge to the understanding of God (or gods) surrounding a sacred site or country. Jesus encountered such beliefs.

For example, the temple at Jerusalem had a considerable amount of 'local' theology attached to it which was derived either from its position in Israel or from its traditions and practices. The very word 'Jerusalem' means a place where the peace of God dwells.

Jerusalem for the Jewish nation is (and always was) the centre of hopes and dreams. It is a magnet for three monotheistic religions but, at the same time, a place producing a belief system all of its own which cannot be transposed directly elsewhere. There can be few places sacred or secular which do not have associations of this kind. Events of the past and local personalities connected with the spot all produce a history and a theology. Much of this 'theology' may well be based on fable and legend or a combination of events and location, but without it society will lack a sense of place as well as a sense of purpose. In a mobile secularised society such as Britain today, this sense of place seems to be rapidly eroding. If you are unable to look out on the same locations as your forefathers, then you may sense something is missing in your personal history, and so more than one commentator has observed that much which can be understood as a search for meaning is also a 'search for place'.

There is yearning to know where I, as an individual, stand in the process of time, where I come from and, ultimately, where I shall be going. It is a search which comes to the surface, and for which a secularised society has little or no answer.

Was it because of this search for place that the relatives of Joseph (Josh. 24:32) took so long to find a burial site for his revered remains? Much later on, though more through fear of pagan invaders, the monastic followers of St Cuthbert were to wander around with his body until at last he could be given a decent burial. To a shifting society with its mooring ropes somewhat adrift the Christian gospel offers meaning, purpose and a 'sense of place' in the security of God's eternal love. This is what I would describe as good biblical local theology.

The local theology of Swindon could relate to the performances of Swindon Town FC where the secular equivalents of 'faith, symbol, worship, hope, community, myth', etc., are easily discernible. The recent history of the club may well indeed illustrate such 'equivalents'. Promoted to the Premier Division in 1993 after winning a thrilling 'play off' final at Wembley, talk of Europe, etc., losing their inspiring player/manager to another club, then to finish bottom of the Premier League, to relegation with a hundred goals let in the net, these ups-and-down can all feed the ideas of hope and disappointment. Unfulfilled dreams and faith, although unrewarded, in the shape of the 'instant heaven' of the Premier League still persist despite the drop to Division One.

A year or two earlier accusations of financial irregularity surrounded the club and, although the team actually won promotion, they were cruelly denied it by the Football League. The team were actually *demoted* to Division 3, and so it was no wonder that the town sprouted many a poster proclaiming 'Div. 1 not Div. 3'. The cynic might argue that that particular demand has now been fulfilled. If a 'theology' like this surrounds a football club, its financial dealings, the team and its performances, so also it must be true for much of the rest of the town and its varied inhabitants.

In Akers Way itself such beliefs and practices might well be seen in connection with the site of St Mary's church itself and its relation to the community. Whether or not that community makes any contribution to support the physical wellbeing of the fabric of the building or the ministry offered within and outside its walls is of little consequence. However, the church does lend considerable symbolic significance to the Christian presence in the community and this is a weighty argument for the traditions regarding the parish system of the Church of England.

Much 'local' theology is, of course, related to the local culture and morale. The closure of the railway works in Swindon in 1986 had a considerable effect on people's lives and beliefs. At its peak the works employed some 18,000 people and had been the real reason for the existence of Swindon for over a hundred years. The works was the supplier and sustainer of thousands of people over many decades. The hospital, chapel, housing and welfare services showed Victorian philanthropy at its best, generated of course by beliefs of a paternalistic God who could supply the needs, and most of the wants, of compliant and dutiful citizens. Although the work-force had been in decline for several years the final 'hooter' in 1986 marked the 'death knell' of an industry which had ruled several generations of Swindonians. The advent of other employers in the 'boom' years of the 1980s was no substitute for the railway works. They provided a range of employment opportunities but they could never match the 'railway age'. Not for nothing was 'GWR' known as 'God's Wonderful Railway'.

It is true that by 1986 Swindon had long since ceased to be a 'one industry' town but beliefs especially of a paternalistic nature can continue long after the original benefactor has disappeared.

The idea of the employer caring for the employee virtually from 'the cradle to the grave' has for the most part disappeared. Working practices and conditions may well have improved dramatically in this century but employers (especially if they are multinationals), although beneficient, can at the same time, be remote and less aware of the effects on the local community. Swindon does have many firms who have considerable concern within the community but it is of a different order than the railway works once offered. It is, of course, an open question as to which pattern had enlightened self-interest at heart rather than the care and welfare of employees. The degree of loyalty generated by the railway works can perhaps be exaggerated but GWR abides as an endearing folk memory in the minds of many in Swindon despite the huge increase in population in successive waves after the Second World War.

Where do local theology and folk religion interact or coincide? Despite the secular nature of society, except for weddings, the demand for 'occasional offices' by the community on the local church shows only a small decline and may well be greater in the future given population increases in many urban areas.

The need for 'rites of passage' is one which psychologists and sociologists may argue about but, in reality, is something to which most ministers in urban areas have given considerable time and attention regardless of the beliefs (or lack of them) of those wishing to participate in them.

The post-Christian secularised society has no credal statement to fall back on but has a compendium of beliefs and myths which from time to time give rise to public expression. In the case of Akers Way these can be summarised in terms of morality, e.g. behaviour of drivers along the road; in terms of authority, commonly held views regarding the local Council and its responsibility in traffic and road safety measures; in terms of fear and prejudice with the 'demonising' of certain individuals who were seen to be at fault. When such attitudes arise the Christian gospel of love, forgiveness and reconciliation will be seen as a disadvantage until emotions retire and a healing process begins.

Swindon's local history

'A northern town set in southern England' was the memorable phrase used to describe to me Wiltshire's largest conurbation. Until about 1840 it had a population of around 2,000 and was, in fact, smaller than several other towns near by, notably Marlborough and Salisbury. Now it numbers more than 160,000 with more to come! There are really only two words to describe the reason for the bulk of this dramatic growth, and those two words are 'The Railway'. If Isambard Kingdom Brunel had not accepted the advice of his young engineer, Daniel Gooch, and therefore decided to site the Great Western Railway's engine and carriage works, as well as the fuelling and refreshment stop on the main line from London to Bristol then, in turn, Swindon would not have developed as it did, nor become a railway legend for many decades.

The most common explanation for choosing Swindon was the fact that it was equidistant in terms of locomotive power between the capital and Bristol. The provision of a large level area and the junction with the line to Gloucester may well also have had an influence in the decision.

But Victorian Swindon was not all built on the god of steam. A canal, built in 1810, had existed before the railway came and later on within Swindon itself, from 1904 there was an extensive tram service. On 1 June 1906, it provided a disaster of the same magnitude as was to occur two miles away some eighty-five years later. At the foot of Victoria Road, which linked the old and new towns of Swindon, a runaway tram derailed and crashed on to its side. There were eventually five fatalities with many injuries. A huge crowd gathered and before nine o'clock that evening a local photographer was selling postcards depicting the horrific scene. Compensation paid by the company amounted to £24,404. The only reminders of this tragic accident are the photographs taken at the time; there is no memorial at the exact spot.

Other tragedies were to follow . . .

During the Second World War, in August 1942, there were several air raids on Swindon in one of which twenty-five people were killed, and in another there were eight fatalities among the civilian population.

Post-war Swindon was to change yet again, though, as its role as a London overspill meant a huge expansion to the roads of the town. The 1960s and 1970s were again marked by large growth so that today's population is now eighty times more than when Brunel came to visit.

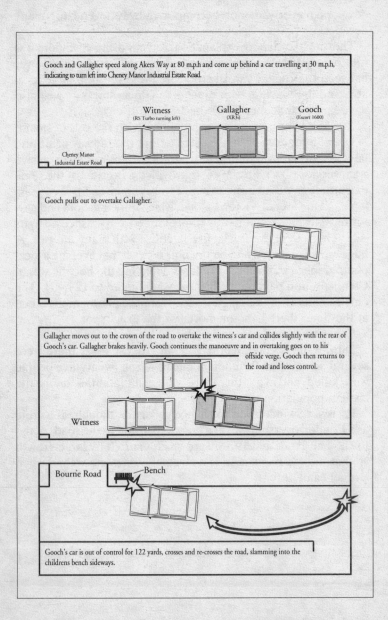

Gooch and Gallagher speed along Akers Way at 80 m.p.h and come up behind a car travelling at 30 m.p.h, indicating to turn left into Cheney Manor Industrial Estate Road.

Witness
(RS Turbo turning left)

Gallagher
(XR3i)

Gooch
(Escort 1600)

Cheney Manor
Industrial Estate Road

Gooch pulls out to overtake Gallagher.

Gallagher moves out to the crown of the road to overtake the witness's car and collides slightly with the rear of Gooch's car. Gallagher brakes heavily. Gooch continues the manoeuvre and in overtaking goes on to his offside verge. Gooch then returns to the road and loses control.

Witness

Bourne Road   Bench

Gooch's car is out of control for 122 yards, crosses and re-crosses the road, slamming into the childrens bench sideways.

**Plan of Akers Way accident – 13 SEPTEMBER 1991
(reproduced from *Swindon Evening Advertiser*)**

Akers Way, Swindon, looking east from site of accident

Akers Way, Swindon, looking west from St Mary's church tower

3

What crisis?

In the course of his or her service most clergy will have to minister to people in situations of trauma. It may mean, at the very least, taking the funeral of an accident victim or victims, or a cot death; it may mean the sudden and unexpected loss of a member of his or her own family; it may mean a whole clutch of events which, because of their unpredictability, complexity and trauma, means the Christian leader might well be pitched into situations for which they are ill suited or equipped to minister. There is, of course, an important subtle difference between feeling ill-equipped and actually being incompetent in such situations. Indeed, it is widely recognised that, even if it is not apparent to others, and certainly not communicated to those immediately in the vicinity, some sense of inadequacy is vital for how else can the individual Christian rely on his or her Lord whatever the situation may be?

However, over the last few years there has been a trend towards a greater 'professionalism' in the ordained ministry for which the church and society as a whole should be grateful. When I compare my own theological college training, where the five staff had a total experience of only six curacies between them, and the now well established pattern of each theological college having an experienced director of pastoral studies, we can see how, at one level clergy skills should have improved.

Because he or she is often local and focal (and maybe vocal) there is much more than just an offering of religious rites and then cessation of further involvement.

The evening of Friday 13 September 1991 was a warm and balmy one, it was as if summer was, on this occasion, not willing to give way to the rigours of autumn. Akers Way, Swindon, is a wide stretch of road with a large greensward and a cycle track and path on the southern side and on the northern side some large verges and banking with footpath. It is only after some 600 yards west from the church that any houses are situated near the road. The speed limit at the time was 40 m.p.h. On this beautiful evening several children sat on a metal seat near, but not adjacent, to the road. It is as safe a place as anywhere and it was somewhere youngsters had congregated since the houses were built and occupied in the late 1950s.

A few yards away, on the opposite side of the road, is a turning to Cheney Manor Industrial Estate. It is, (or was), a simple 'T' junction with clear sight lines along the main road. A car prepares to turn left into the estate, another car travelling at speed anticipates the manoeuvre, moves out a little into the centre of the road, whilst another following car travelling even faster attempts to overtake the second car which is now the middle vehicle. In so doing the third car brushes the second car and then veers sharply to the right, turns on to its right hand side into the bench on which the youngsters were sitting killing three outright, fatally injuring two others, and seriously injuring another two.

It is, indeed a crisis for the families involved, the emergency services, the community, the local council(s) the administration of justice. the local church and the media. How would each cope? A minister at the Hillsborough disaster was reported as saying 'The only thing we can do is weep'. Certainly the biblical injunction to 'weep with those who weep' (Romans 12:15) is very much part of Christian ministry in such situations but surely there is much more the church can contribute not least in the teaching of reconciliation, forgiveness, and healing where there is such great hurt.

The fact this crisis was very local meant (and still means) that its ministry was limited to a small area. All the victims including those who recovered lived within a mile of each other and five of them within a few hundred yards of each other. The drivers of the cars involved might well have been known by the victims' families as they, too, came from the same area. Unlike (say) The Herald of Free Enterprise (1987) or the Tenerife Runway crash (1977) the pain, although just as deep was, of course, nothing like as widespread. Nevertheless, for those involved, it was probably the biggest crisis they had ever faced. Throughout twenty-five years in the Anglican ministry I have been involved in ministry to the relatives of suicides, holiday accidents, fire deaths, industrial accidents and so on, but coping with so many at once was, indeed, a stretching of both spiritual, mental and physical resources. The fact that I worked in a team meant, of course, that the load was shared and some of the other work was undertaken by others, for which I shall always be grateful.

Because of the delays of couples coming for wedding interviews and wedding rehearsals in church, my arrival at the scene was some half an hour after the crash. 'There are at least three dead' was the police inspector's first comment as she immediately left what she was doing to come and speak to me. There then followed a busy, confusing and demanding evening, at the end of which others, including the local full-time hospital chaplains as well as the emergency services must have felt much more drained than myself. Nevertheless, being rung at 1.45 a.m. by the press, having just got to bed, did not help restore one's nervous energy! Later on I shall reflect on the responsibility of the media in reporting such events.

Alan Billings in his reflection on his involvement in the Hillsborough disaster[3] says that though he had seen death many times in the course of his twenty years in the ministry 'this caught me out'. He reflects that it may be the combination of the intensity of feelings, the sheer numbers involved, the speed at which events happened or that those hurt and killed were so young, that made him feel unprepared.

'Lord, help us to expect the unexpected' is a prayer that my wife and I pray some mornings – perhaps we should do it more often! Whether or not we did so on the morning of Friday 13 September 1991, or not I cannot now remember. Certainly, by strange design, when we don't pray that, the unexpected always seems to happen!

In other cultures with less of a Christian background, the interpretation of the event, as well as preparedness for it, may take a different guise. Even so, in our post-Christian society the fact that the crash occurred on Friday the 13th caused speculation of a fatalistic nature. There is some evidence that a few of the grieving families, who were all of Anglo-Saxon working-class background, did consult less orthodox sources for care and counsel. Since all of them were well established in the area with a considerable network of family, workplace and neighbourhood ties this obviously meant they had some contact with people of spiritualist or fringe-religion beliefs. It would seem also to be true that in our society, despite its sophistications and secular outlook, superstition dies hard. So there were no lack of resources, both offered and sought, which proffered some form of hope and comfort. It may well be a case of 'any port in a storm' and a desperate search for meaning on the part of those who are in the depths of despair. It is very easy for Christians all too quickly to condemn such quests, but certainly from a biblical standpoint they stand out as erroneous in both doctrine and practice. Yet, when people, especially from a secular working-class background, are thrown into turmoil by a disaster of such magnitude, then it should come as no surprise that hope of this kind is considered and sought.

The fact that in many cases the number 13 is avoided when houses are numbered, and by footballers on the sub-bench, and that a whole host of other vague beliefs and practices still hold sway in our society, is some evidence that the process of secularisation has not been as universally adopted as is sometimes thought. For many people this superstition is, it seems, largely subliminal and only emerges at crisis times. For others it is very much a way of life.

It is too sweeping a statement to say Britain is a superstitious country; any casual glance or observation will produce much to prove this is not true. Nevertheless, people who are not committed Christians (and indeed a few who are!) will offer less than rational explanations to calamitous events, and often indulge in such superstitions as throwing salt over their shoulder, avoid walking under ladders, as well as a minor cluster of beliefs regarding the four days in the year when Friday and the thirteenth of the month coincide.

It is a point of some debate as to whether it is a secular rational culture or the effects of centuries of Christian teaching that keep such beliefs and practices to the relatively low level they appear to be.

Much effort, in recent years, has gone into preparing major disaster plans. The emergency services must always be prepared.

There is not only the need to meet the demands of the immediate situation but, because of public scrutiny by the media and later by statutory enquiry, the very best course of action needs to be taken. Of course, the circumstances in which the emergency services have to work are, in reality, often far from ideal, e.g. the Kings Cross tube station fire. Careful planning may well be advanced for a major event, but what happens when the disaster does not fit into that category? The accident referred to throughout this book had unpredictability (the chances of it happening can be estimated at millions to one), accountability (in that criminal charges ensued), trauma, political action, ritual and local community involvement. In addition to the six families of those killed and injured, it involved the families of the three drivers, three local schools, all within several hundred yards of the site, the local parish church and members of various community groups. In all it must have affected (and still affects), either directly or indirectly, the lives of possibly 10,000 people out of an Anglican parish population of 23,000 and the population of Swindon as a whole of 140,000. These figures might seem small when compared with Lockerbie, for example, but they were dramatic enough for those concerned.

The parochial system of the Church of England has always meant that it has been in a unique position with regard to the pastoral care of those committed to its charge. Whilst the trend in recent years has been to focus on the inner life of the congregation with its real emphasis on being the body of Christ, not just a gathering of the disparate faithful, nevertheless, when major or minor crises arise if this trend is emphasised too much, there can be little to offer to the outsider. At this point one cannot help comparing the involvement of the Church of England with that of the local Exclusive Brethren assembly whose meeting hall is very near Akers Way, and whose children attended all three local schools. Emphasis on the internal life of their church is set over and against any local community involvement. Perhaps too, a theology of God's judgement on an evil world is felt to take precedence over pastoral care for victims of a road accident, when, as in this case, none were members of any Christian community still less of their particular sect.

In my own case, of the six families directly involved, I only knew one in any meaningful way, since I had taken the wedding of the boys' widowed father and their stepmother twelve months previously. It was they who made a direct request to see me in the hospital the night of the accident. Of the others, my wife, through her involvement in one of the local schools, knew the two youngest who were killed and the mother, brother and sisters of one of those children. None of those directly hurt were, at the time, worshipping members of the local church though all would claim, in some way to be 'C of E'.

However, it was also a crisis for the local Christian community and, in later chapters, I shall attempt to spell out what it meant to the congregation of St Mary's, Rodbourne Cheney. Whilst crisis management should be a necessary part of the training of clergy, it is hardly possible to prepare the local church as a whole. The spiritual health of the congregation does, however have a real bearing on how its members may or may not respond in a crisis situation, and whether that response is honouring to God and 'Kingdom extending' in its actions.

No discussion of response to a crisis can be complete without some mention of personal crises in individual lives. As I recalled in Chapter 1, both my wife and I have known the experience of widowhood, and only twelve months before the Akers Way accident my own father had died choking on a sandwich whilst watching cricket. How do clergy cope with disaster when something similar may be happening to them personally? The value of clergy teams (whatever their drawbacks) obviously comes to the fore in such circumstances. But, if the individual minister knows how to cope with the threat of ministerial 'burn out', has good powers of delegation, is able to relax under stress and knows his or her limitations, then his or her contribution will be a help not a hindrance.

It is an obvious truism that a more mobile population which is increasing in density makes the chances of man-made disasters more likely, yet human nature is such that few live on 'tenter hooks' waiting for it to happen. Preparedness there may be in the emergency services, but it seems to end there, for few live as though this day will be their last. The warnings of Jesus in Matthew 24 are largely ignored by many Christians.

At times, specific Christian ministerial help may not be welcome. At the 1986 Lockington rail crash in which nine people died, the local vicar was on the scene within a short while, only to be told to leave. After considerable correspondence and some media attention, a recognised plan was drawn up in which local clergy have a small but significant part.

All Christian leaders have, at some stage, to deal with grief and pain, both within their own families but, more especially, within the church and community. It may only rarely be sudden in their own lives but with some 10,000 fatal accidents in any one year, such events are common in Christian ministry. Indeed, in the parish in which I serve, there were at least three accidental deaths in the twelve months following the Akers Way tragedy. Only rarely do these incidents involve larger numbers, but some kind of preparedness and training does seem to be vital. At one of the funerals for the victims of 13 September, 1991, I was asked, 'What kind of training have you had for all this?' I replied, 'None at all, only twenty-four years' experience of full-time ministry'. When I reflect on that answer I recognise something of my own inadequacies and, looking back, see some mistakes that could have been avoided, as well as wondering how I would have coped had I been less experienced and on my own in the parish.

The public confidence of a Christian has often been likened to a swan gliding across a lake. All calm on the exterior whilst paddling furiously unseen beneath the water. In this sense the Christian leader should be no different to other professionals involved in traumatic circumstances. Some clergy, of course, have used the resources of their own personal counsellor to fall back upon. For my own part I have never found this necessary. Whatever the human resources in such situations there must always be the relationship with and reliance on the One who knows the situation far better than anyone else and whose Spirit can do more than we can ever ask or expect.

Remains of the seat on which the children were sitting
(Reproduced with permission from *Swindon Evening Advertiser*)

Shaun Gooch's car after the accident
(Reproduced with permission from *Swindon Evening Advertiser*)

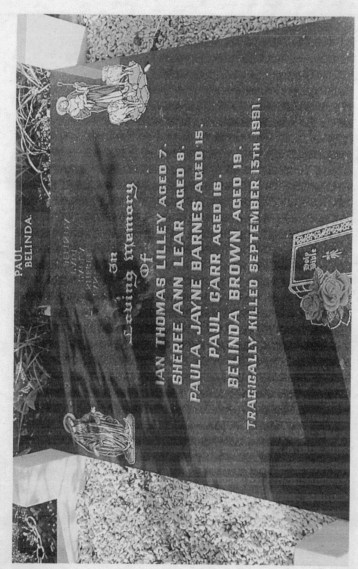

Memorial stone in Akers Way, Swindon

4

Expecting the Unexpected

Much has already been written about some of the deficiencies and inadequacies in full-time ministry training in coping with traumatised situations, both of small, medium and large scale – those with a national or international dimension such as Lockerbie, and those with a local impact such as the Akers Way accident. John Harris in *Stress, Power and Ministry* states, 'The question of competency remains a profoundly troubling one for pastors and the church as a whole'.[4] Although great efforts have been made to improve clergy training in recent years certainly the public image of clergy is still very much that of the vicar in, say, the television programme *Dad's Army* or of Trollope's vicars in the novels set in Barchester. We can be glad that Britain, on the whole, does not suffer from anti-clericalism, but, as yet, we have still to see a TV series where the clergy are portrayed with the professionalism of an Inspector Morse.

Harris, along with others, gives at least four reasons which helped fuel this ministry crisis. First, there was the fact that psychotherapists and behavioural science practitioners took over the traditional role of pastoral care. Secondly, basic shifts in our views of reality have undercut traditional images of God. Harris was, of course, writing not so long after the 'Death of God' theology came very much to the fore. The emergence of the renewal movement, both within and without mainstream churches, seems to have dealt some heavy blows to this kind of extreme theology. The 'Death of God' movement, however, has yet to die. Spending some time at a theological college in 1991 I found, to my surprise, more than one student about to be ordained, who seemed to have little idea of their vocation and ministry. Maybe they are the exception but they still seem to exist.

The third reason Harris gives is that clergy were ill-prepared for the stunning variety of values and ideologies that have emerged in society. Harris was, of course, referring to the moral and religious scene in the USA but in that land, at least, the percentage of church-goers and public expression of belief are much higher than in the UK.

Lastly, Harris questions the concept of parish leadership as taught in seminaries, at least in the 1970s. Harris goes on to say that in any given situation three things stand out.

(1) *Self-acceptance*. 'There must be confidence in self, for only then can I value others.' I would want to add that for the committed Christian such confidence is very much tied up with confidence in Christ. Paul wrote, 'There is no condemnation now for those who live in union with Christ Jesus' (Rom. 8:1).

(2) *Confirmation*. 'When others experience me (and presumably value me) then I am able to experience myself and I am able to gauge the effect I have on others'.

(3) *Essentiality*. 'The greater I am able to use my central abilities . . . the greater will be my feelings of essentiality to myself and the setting in which I am involved.'

Harris does add a fourth requirement which he entitles 'Realisation of self-knowledge' (which must, in fact, be tied up with self-acceptance). Self-knowledge is about the style of ministry and the use of power and weakness both in oneself and in others.

Peter Rudge has identified three styles of ministry relating to the ability not only to cope but to fulfil a worthwhile role, only one of which he says is truly biblical.[5] In the first of these patterns of ministry there are those who are concerned with maintaining the 'status quo'. They may rely on constitutions, creeds or doctrinal formulas which, if they are not careful, become the sole reason for their ministry. The foundations may well be laudable in motive and biblical in character but they feel threatened when the spirit of change is abroad. If society around them is conservative and stable, then they are at their most comfortable. Such ministers would be truly happy with the line in the hymn which says 'For nothing changes here'. At best it is a sub-biblical attitude, at worst it queries the Spirit of God.

Another style which Rudge identifies is that of the 'representative' ministry. The priest is the local, focal person and the Anglican system has at its best given credence to this view-point. The minister may well represent the congregation to the local pub as well as in church synods and boards but does this really fulfil his or her vocation?

Now, of course, both these examples might well exist in the same person, whereas the third example is the 'facilitator for change' model which Rudge argues is the more biblical and, therefore, more compatible with Christian values. It, of course, contains elements of the prophetic voice and it must be admitted this can sometimes be seen within structural organisations. On the other hand the 'facilitator for change' may be more of a John the Baptist figure working outside the establishment bringing a questioning voice to bear upon its methods and attitudes.

The 'facilitator for change' is also best able to cope with personal change in his or her own life and in the lives of others. As a pastor he or she is seen as responding to the needs of others. As evangelist he or she is seen as the agent of change in the hearts and minds of those hearing (and responding to) the gospel.

On a personal note, I am grateful to have absorbed some of this teaching several years ago and, whilst not claiming the 'gift of prophecy' in the generally understood 'charismatic' sense, would claim that the radical cutting edge to ministry is part of my brief whilst at times I am required to be representative and also a part of an established church with the aura of 'status quo' which that entails.

Rudge offers in one case a view of management in the Church that is mechanistic and shows little consideration for others. It is on the whole impersonal. The Church is seen as an organisation simply to be managed. If each person in the organisation has a clear role and function to play, then all will be well. It is efficient, effective but without much of a soul! How different from Jesus's style of managing people.

As a contrast to this there is a 'classic' view of management in the ministry which takes a totally opposite position. It is inefficient and wasteful of both human and other resources. It may be pious, but lacks the skills to shape and change the world or refashion the Church. It may be in tune with God but it forgets the world is singing a different song!

The best model, Rudge suggests, is an 'organic system'. If one is to be sensitive to the nature of the church, one needs to look in the field of management for something that is consonant with this nature. The importance of the organic view of management is that it is couched in the same idiom as much of New Testament theology about the church, particularly the passages which refer to it as the body of Christ. This emphasis in the New Testament is reinforced by the way in which Christ drew upon the world of nature for many of his parables about the kingdom of God. It may come as a surprise to find that there has developed in the hard world of business a point of view which has such close affinity with Christian experience, with an understanding of the nature of the Church and with a strategy for it expressed in terms of the renewal of charism: '. . . It is unlikely that the development of the organic view of management sprang from a theological conversion of industrialists. They are more likely to have been prompted by a desire to respond to a rapidly changing world – circumstances very similar to those which the Church is facing.'[5]

So the effective minister is neither a dominating overlord nor a subservient underling but one who brings gifts of leadership (which will often be misunderstood). Charism will be tested to the full in a crisis situation.

Given that a local or national crisis may occur in any one parish and given widely differing styles of churchmanship, experience and ability to cope, added to the fact that the professionalism of the clergy rarely exceeds that of the emergency services, and can compare unfavourably with that of the police or fire brigade, it is not surprising to have heard a few local clergy say following the Akers Way crash, 'I'm glad it was you and not me'. It is necessary not only to be able to cope but to make sure, at the very least, that the public image of God's church (already a confused one in many people's eyes) is maintained and not harmed.

Although I write this from within an unashamed evangelical framework I would be the first to acknowledge that the gospel of Jesus Christ is much broader than is normally portrayed within the evangelical wing of the Church of England and among evangelicals elsewhere.

Under this broad framework four areas need to be addressed:

(a) training. We need to know how to act in an emergency.
(b) support. We need to consider from where it is likely to come.
(c) debriefing, telling the tale, after-care and counselling the counsellors.
(d) after-effects, both short, medium and long-term.

Training

After theological college the new minister is subject to a number of years post-ordination training which may differ in quality from diocese to diocese but which, in my judgement, has rapidly improved over recent years. After that, further opportunities are, on the whole, a matter of personal choice from a variety of conferences available, and clergy postbags are often bulging with such events.

Attendance at diocesan sponsored training will be particularly encouraged and money will be made available for study leave and annual training grants. Many parishes, though by no means all, also make money available for such further training. However, it is often up to the individual minister to make sure it happens. Much of the substance of this writing was done during sabbatical leave but it did need a great deal of tenacity and patience before I could be certain that time and finance would be available to achieve what I envisaged. Compulsion, at least within the orders of the Anglican Church, has never been a strong point; every incumbent is seen as 'king' or 'queen' in his or her own parish so what is often a strength in one area is also a weakness when it comes to making sure levels of competence are kept up or even improved.

For centuries Anglican clergy have had 'job security' in what is known a 'freehold'. It meant in most cases almost a 'job for life' and still requires considerable legal effort to remove clergy who abuse this privilege. But there is now a great increase in contracted posts the outlook of the supremo vicar is certainly being eroded. Financial difficulties in all churches, with the laity being asked to contribute more to 'quotas', will almost certainly mean that before long there will be great expectation of 'value for money' in full-time ministry.

The question of answerability will certainly come to the fore but to whom, in precise terms, is the local Anglican minister accountable? The bishop? Yes, that has in one sense always been true, but now the clergy will be seen more and more to be accountable to the local church simply because its members are paying most if not all of his or her stipend.

As far as I can discover, there is very little being done in the area of both the theology of collaborative ministry as well as in understanding its dynamics. The collegiality of the team when this accident occurred owed much to the grace of God in drawing together both the ordained ministry and the church members. Such collegiality does, however, mean much more than polite co-operation. It means in reality being able truly to support each other in a way and style which counteracts what has often been taught and practised in the past.

Certainly it must be true that clergy are less isolationist than they were, say twenty or thirty years ago but old images and habits die hard. I am not putting a case forward for the scrapping of the Anglican parish system even where the word 'parish' is only related to ecclesiastical boundaries and is not meaningful for example, to many wedding couples and baptism enquirers. I dread the day when the Church of England has only the diocese and deanery as its structures. However, I would argue that we should not wait until a crisis occurs, or financial pressures demand it, for a radical look at clergy relationships.

The petty jealousies and subtle, or not so subtle verbal warfare of Barchester might well have gone but what has replaced it? More is needed than being nice, kind and understanding of one's partners in the gospel.

On a personal note, and as I recounted earlier in Chapter 1, when I moved north in 1982 to work in a team after more than nine years in a sole incumbency, it came as a shock to have to lead and work alongside three other clergy. Especially as I later discovered that the wife of one of them had applied for my post on behalf of her husband!

Induction training for clergy is minimal. Getting square pegs into square holes is an art form which bishops and patrons often attempt to carry out with great care and skill but, in my judgement, still too much is left to chance. More thought needs to be given to situations where clergy are not only expected to work together but in crisis management have to collaborate to a very great degree.

During our sabbatical leave, it was a joy and privilege for my wife and I to worship together in at least fifteen churches both within the Anglican fold and without. Leaving aside matters of churchmanship, numbers, decor and weather, the standards varied enormously from the very good to the very bad. If this happens within liturgy and worship the same must be true to a great degree of pastoral care. Are we guilty of accepting low standards in God's Church and its professional ministry which would not be tolerated in, for example, the police or the fire brigade?

Of course the Church is a body of volunteers and accordingly there must be tolerance and love for those who do not conform to what might be deemed 'middle-class' standards. Nevertheless, God is a God of order not chaos and *as long as the order does not restrain God's vibrant active Spirit then it is to be welcomed*. However, all too often Christians get immersed not in Christ but in a system where flexibility, adaptability and change are viewed with suspicion and disbelief. Not that such movements are the same thing or always right, but often ultra-conservative viewpoints cause the debate to be stillborn before a reasonable case for change can be put. As I reflect on changes in liturgy and ministry in the Church of England in the past thirty years they can often be seen to be reactive rather than proactive. Much of Jesus's ministry would seem to fall in the latter category. John 3:16 is about God *loving* the world. God is the initiator not just One responding to crises as they occur.

The question we are dealing with here is how that body and particularly its leaders can cope with a major crisis on its doorstep. A disaster can happen anywhere but, in Britain at least, it will take place in someone's parish. Lockerbie was a small Scottish town which only a limited number of people knew about. Aberfan likewise was a Welsh mining town known only by a relatively small number of people. Yet now these names will for ever be associated with the tragedies that befell them. I doubt very much if the local clergy at the time had any special training for the task that was suddenly imposed on them. It is a deficiency which in part, but only in part, can now be rectified.

Yet, if the majority of students leaving college for full-time ministry are competent, efficient and publicly acceptable then there should be a reasonable degree of competence in crisis, no matter how weak and ineffective the minister (male or female) may feel. It is one of those situations where godliness is not enough. The Anglican situation means a ministry to all. At the same time ministry to people on the margins of God's church does not have to be ill-defined in theology or practice. To my mind, the weakness of God's church and especially its ordained ministry is not shown up by the odd scandal which the tabloid press will exploit but by the inefficiency and incompetence of the local cleric in his or her public role. The problem, it seems, lies in answerability. Once a minister is past the probationary period of, say, a first curacy there is little that can be done to raise standards. Goals about 'in-service' training and sabbaticals might be very welcome in diocesan circles but, in the end, it often comes down to a matter of individual desire and choice. There is, of course, accountability in the matter of moral behaviour, and canon law lays down some expectations of the minimal norm, but it can do nothing to change the ineffective into the effective, the lazy into the diligent, the inefficient into the efficient, and so on.

When I was ordained in the mid-1960s not a few of my brother clergy seemed reincarnations of Parson Woodforde[6] whose diaries (1759–1802) reflect both the England of his day and an Anglican Church in its spiritual doldrums. The ordained ministry, he portrays all about form and rules; about saying prayers and being part of the social round; about talking about 'my people' and enjoying a security of tenure but having little spiritual drive or realistic goals. Thankfully within a century the preaching of Wesley and Whitefield, and the Anglo-Catholic revival were to bring significant changes but, in the Church of England, old attitudes die a very slow death. How, I wonder, would Parson Woodforde have coped with the crisis of the seriousness of the Akers Way tragedy.

Of course, when the minister is responsible both to his or her ecclesiastical superiors *and* some other authority, then standards of action are often much higher. Witness the recorded talk on TV by the chaplain to the Parachute Regiment in the Falklands conflict, witness the way most hospital and prison chaplains perform their ministry partly, I suspect, not only because of their particular gifts, but because they are answerable to an authority additional to the Church into which they were ordained.

A 'major' incident is often defined as one where there are, or there are likely to be, seven or more fatalities. Some incidents fall easily into this category, e.g. the terrorist bombing at Enniskillen, Northern Ireland, on Remembrance Day. Others are less easy to define, not so much in terms of fatalities since any one unnatural death is a 'major' incident in the lives of those concerned, but on the degree of devastation and damage that have been caused. Generally, it is the responsibility of the police to define what is 'major' and what is not. Subsequent events may, of course, convert a relatively minor event into a major catastrophe.

What then is being done in terms of clergy training for such events? In the course of the writing of this book, a number of theological colleges, directors of pastoral studies and directors of post-ordination training were contacted in order to learn their views in response to the question: 'Are your students aware of the existence of major incident plans for the county in which they will work or (in the case of those newly ordained) where they work already?'

Most replied that there was little awareness of such plans, which is perhaps understandable in the case of the theological colleges, but only Southwark diocese said that post-ordination training (POT) students were 'very aware of such plans and what their role might be within such plans'. The reasons for this can be summed up in two ways. The pressure to include items in training programmes is very high and not all can be accommodated; secondly there seems to be a gap between *ad hoc* training and that required for any formal major incident plan.

The point I am wishing to stress in this chapter is not that gaps exist in the training of clergy – understandably so in the case of theological colleges, less so with regard to continuing ministerial education and POT – but that on the night of 13 September 1991, my colleagues and I were unprepared for the incident we had to face. However, as events proved, hopefully we were not ill-equipped to deal with the liturgical and pastoral needs, as they suddenly erupted.

It might well be argued that because such incidents are rare and because the role of the clergy in *major* incidents will eventually have widespread recognition, it can be left to the local clergy to deal with as best they can. Surely if the good standing of God's Church and, more importantly, the needs of the dying, bereaved and injured, are at stake, then it cannot be left to *ad hoc* training, but should be included in training under the heading of something like 'Expecting the Unexpected'.

Finally, it is worth noting that in 1994 the government allocated £76 million for emergency planning, but rejected calls for legislation compelling councils to draw up disaster plans.

In 1983 when I became Area Dean of East Hull I found that, should I escape nuclear attack, part of my responsibilities would be to head up a local survival committee in the event of an explosion over the city. No one told me who would be responsible should I not survive, nor exactly what my role ought to be! Was this God's way of urging me to be prepared at some future point in ministry to 'Expect the Unexpected'? It is difficult to speculate, but with the fading possibility of nuclear warfare, perhaps also we are failing to prepare ourselves for other lesser disasters as well.

5

By what authority?

The title 'cure of souls' is perhaps a strange one to many people. It speaks of a past when the Church of England in its local clergy was much more influential in matters of the Spirit and indeed in temporal affairs. To a large extent it still holds true despite the presence of other religions and denominations and not least despite the secularism and materialism of our times. The Church of England is still the established church and may well be for decades to come. Yet the role of the local clergy has been marginalised in many areas. For all that the vicar is still the vicar i.e. the vicarious one who speaks (and sometimes suffers) on behalf of others. Four aspects of this particular ministry became apparent in the time following the accident and since.

Vicarious ministry for the families

No, I was not the spokesman who spoke to the media on behalf of the families. No, I did not represent them in any formal or legal way but I could represent them before God. I could try to enter their pain and heartache. I could attempt to answer some of the questions raised about their needs. However, it would be invidious to suggest that this was a ministry where I operated alone; many others were involved but, as team rector, obviously a greater responsibility fell upon my shoulders.

I knew none of the bereaved families before the accident, though they may have recognised me, and in my judgement the best forms of ministry arise out of a long-term caring relationship. These days, when faced with an ever-increasing population and falling numbers of full-time clergy, it is a ministry (at least initially) between strangers. To emphasise the point, how many non-Christians actually know someone who worships regularly? Significant numbers of young couples, when asked this or a similar question during marriage preparation, state quite categorically that they know no one who is a committed Christian. (This has huge implications for outreach in the Decade of Evangelism let alone for pastoral care).

Certainly Jesus's ministry was very much to the outsider: the blind, the leper, the lame who were not part of the apostolic group. But also we find the comment, 'He could not do any miracles there [his home town], except lay his hands on a few . . .' (Mark 6:5). Even Jesus, in a situation where He was well known, had a limited ministry.

The most effective setting for Christian ministry is a 'faith to faith' situation, i.e. combined trust in God between the minister (ordained or not) and another Christian. This might be the most attractive scenario to work within but it has never been the starting point for Anglican ministry which sets out to treat all people as Christians unless proved otherwise. The next best scenario would seem to be where a relationship has already been firmly established at some time in the past, and the person now inviting and accepting ministry although not a believer knows the minister in some way.

Sadly the other pattern is where relationships need to be established very quickly in order that the love of God may operate effectively. This is an area which needs considerable further exploration but is often the norm in today's secular society where Christian 'rites of passage' are still in very great demand. A stranger will take the funeral of a loved one, a stranger will preside at a wedding, a stranger will take the baptism of your children. Yes, there may have been visits and preparation beforehand but it is rarely out of a long-term relationship that such events take place. The vicar is not the family friend he (or she) once was. It is on the whole no fault of him or her but largely a result of the disparity of numbers. Obviously one person can only know a certain number of people at any one time, generally of the order of 250/300. How can they know 10,000? In 1962 the population of England and Wales was 42 million with some 16,000 Anglican clergy. In the latter half of the twentieth century the proportion is very different. It is in the order of a population of 44 million with some 10,500 Anglican clergy. The number of church weddings and baptisms may have declined but there is still a huge demand by the non-churchgoing public for the services of the clergy for such 'rites of passage'. The welcome and biblical rise in the ministry of the laity has done very little to dent or divert this demand. The vicar is still the local focal person (or parson) whom most people see only at such events.

Vicarious ministry in and for the community

During the events of September 1991, and afterwards, there was an obvious need for someone who could speak on behalf of the community. In the parish in which I served the community was somewhat ill-defined. Rodbourne Cheney was the ecclesiastical parish containing parts of other communities which had once been hamlets on the edge of Swindon. A question frequently asked by the media on such occasions is, 'What is the community feeling now?' Who was I to answer on behalf of others? By what right could I respond on their behalf? I was not an elected representative. By historical accident the parish was what it was and I guess few would say they knew and belonged to such a parish. Indeed much time is spent in explaining to wedding and baptism couples exactly in which parish they actually live. I have never had any doubt or confusion about my own role in the ordained ministry. It is to be a Christian leader within a congregation of the household of God. But there are many other secondary roles which are often peculiar to Anglican clergy. They bring both obvious advantages and disadvantages. The opportunity for wider contact with people is not to be gainsaid. Being a governor at that time of all three schools involved in the tragedy was one of these wider contacts. The disadvantages of being diverted into subsidiary matters which, although important to the community, are not really part of the gospel, is all too obvious.

Nevertheless, despite the reduced status of clergy in society and the fact that some Christian leaders can feel marginalised, it is often to them that community (and especially the media) will turn in a moment of crisis. This is not a moment for 'taking charge' but for endeavouring to articulate the corporate feelings of others. A locality which has little or no community identity often finds itself to be a community by force of tragedy, and then needs to find someone to speak on its behalf. A community without a secular figurehead will turn in all directions to find some kind of authority. The role of representing the community before God and His Church was an important spiritual one and it was one which I gladly accepted. Prior to coming to Swindon I had always felt it important to play some part in the community either as a school governor or parish councillor. It is a significant means of representing the Christian church (or at least the Anglican part of it) to the wider community and vice versa.

So, although I would always decline the role as 'figurehead', for that mantle needs an authority I do not possess, nevertheless here was an opportunity for leadership and representation which is the privilege of all who are called to service in the ordained ministry.

Vicarious ministry in and for the Christian church

If the leadership role in the wider community was (and is) vague and amorphous, yet of some historical profile, within the local church it is much clearer. Here it is explicitly defined. In New Testament terms it is to be under-shepherd of the flock of Christ. The instructions in 1 Peter 5:2–3 could not be any clearer: 'Be shepherds of God's flock that is under your care, serving as overseers – not because you must, but because you are willing as God wants you to be'. Incidentally, I preached on this text on the evening of the day I was ordained in 1967. Leadership not only involves representing the church to the wider community, it exercises spiritual oversight of those who are committed to Christ and express that allegiance in regular worship.

Learning to lead in this way is always an ongoing process. After several years in my present post more than one person has come to me with the words, 'I have come to see you, Geoffrey, not because you are my rector but because you are my friend' and this demonstrates how relationships can develop. This very delicate area of the relationship between people and pastor is not really my province here. However, if these relationships are of some reasonable quality despite all the weaknesses and failings on both sides, they can be very fruitful and productive when a crisis occurs. It is of paramount importance that the local church should work as a team together for Christ instead of being involved in its own internal squabbles. If this is important for the normal everyday life of the Christian community, how vital it will be when a ghastly incident occurs only 600 yards away from its premises.

In another sense, too, the local Anglican rector can (and should?) vicariously represent God's world-wide Church in both its glories and difficulties. Being a member of the clergy is not an exclusive role and, on a personal level, I do not feel I have ever represented the Church of England (or any Church for that matter) merely as its local representative. If I am able to serve as a school governor or parish councillor, for example, whilst being an incumbent, it demonstrates that these are God's concerns as well and cannot be left exclusively to secular decision-makers, however well-intentioned they may be.

When a major crisis occurs the minister will have the opportunity of being a source of two-way information, not least to stimulate committed Christians to pray and care. In so doing there is (or should be) communion the other way and, whether welcomed or not, a demonstration of the reality of corporate Christian love to the suffering community. It will make great demands in terms of commitment, time, energy, emotions and, not least on good communication skills. It is not an image to be projected for political ends but in order to demonstrate the reality of God's love shown by God's people. If this love is not seen in the leaders of the church where else will it be found?

Vicarious ministry to colleagues

Although there is inevitably some element of loneliness in any leadership role, nevertheless, I praise God for almost all the fellow clergy I have worked with down the years. The dynamic of clergy relationships is a strange one. It hit me quite hard when I took on the job of leading a four-person team ministry after a sole incumbency of nine-and-a-half years. As is often the case I had no real training for such a role. I had gained experience of being a curate in two very diverse places but nowhere had I gained training in being a team-leader. Yet God in His infinite wisdom had prepared me for the role. The role shepherd of the shepherds and leader of the leaders requires oversight but, because clergy are often steeped in a tradition of single leadership, it also means that lessons have to be unlearned, and often very quickly at that. Our team at the time of the accident consisted of a newly-ordained deacon, a lady deacon who had been in the parish only five months, a team vicar who had been here for less than a year and myself who had, by then, been in post three and a half years. However, we did have working alongside us two older semi-retired colleagues and I deeply appreciated their ministry at that particular time and since. 'Leave the routine work to me,' said one of them who had known the parish from childhood days. I shall always be grateful for that offer and its practical implications.

Whatever the legalities of Anglican team ministry it is the relationships between clergy that are so vital. I know God can and will work despite my own great weakness as a professional minister; I know He is not entirely dependent on His full-time workers; far from it but, nevertheless, good team work is essential in any building exercise for His kingdom.

We cannot expect unity in the wider Church if interpersonal relationships in the local leadership are not of the highest order. Yes, God can work despite differences in temperament, background and ability, but when the local Christian leadership is at odds with itself, what hope is there for the Church in the wider world? I am not speaking about ecumenical relationships here, though in many clergy teams this might well be a factor, but, to borrow a phrase from the wedding service, about 'the mutual support and care for each other'. There must be a real desire to keep relationships both honest, with differences not being swept under the carpet, and also caring and supportive. Increasingly there are situations where full-time Christian workers are being stretched as never before with the result that their interpersonal qualities are being stretched in ways previous generations of clergy never knew.

As one bishop put it, 'There are simply no longer any parishes where those who should never have been ordained can be safely hidden'. What is now true for the Church of England has, I guess, been true for much longer in other denominations.

So the biblical style of leadership (outlined in Chapter 4) is vital in any team of clergy. It involves loving, listening, learning and leading in ways which clerics in the past could never have imagined.

Loving Christ

Christian love is always a responsive love: 'He first loved us' (1 John 4:10). Love for God is the first requirement of anyone called to serve in any capacity in what is His church. It is sadly a requirement that is all-too-easily forgotten when personalities clash and outside pressures bear in on His people.

At the time of the accident I thought little about the vicarious nature of my role. As far as I am aware I was not over-protective towards my colleagues nor was I consciously aware of my role as a spokesman on behalf of others. Whilst being team rector of the parish, most people viewed me simply as the 'vicar of St Mary's'.

Looking back on the event itself there was a need for us as a team to study, to weep and pray together, but there was also a need for me to set a lead for others to follow. It was not a particularly lonely role – the sheer speed of events and media interest meant little time to reflect or think, and perhaps knowing how to support other clergy was at times only learnt *en passant*. As three of the four of us had sufficient experience not to be knocked out of our stride there had to be an assumption, on my part, that they could more than cope, especially as I was called upon to be in a much more up-front role than they were.

Nevertheless it was a ministry shared at least in liturgical and ritual terms. However, if my colleagues did need any extra help I probably was not aware of it. The dichotomy of having to minister on two planes at once is not a new feature for those who are called to serve God in full-time leadership.

6

Caring in a crisis

It is now becoming a widely recognised truth, both in law and in the world of medicine, that many of those involved in crisis situations suffer from extensive after-effects. Whilst writing this book, a considerable compensation award was made against London Transport for the consequences experienced by a fire officer involved in the blaze at Kings Cross underground station in 1988. Post-traumatic stress then not only affects victims and their families, but many who care within the orbit of the accident itself.

In this chapter I shall compare some of my own reactions to those of others involved in the Akers Way accident, and in addition refer to descriptions from similar situations and others where there has been an even greater loss of life of the effect of the trauma on caring people and emergency services involved.

For carers in traumatic situations one of the most common after-effects is the nightmare. That nightmare might well be a 'daymare' in the shape of flashbacks during waking hours, perhaps in public or when similar events are witnessed, such as in television news items or a drama series, so-called 'faction' drama might especially trigger the memory of personal stress. Nightmares at least occur in the privacy of the home, but what if the home is a stressful one? Maybe the reaction to events has caused marital breakdown or precipitated violence towards others?

Rev J.M. Shields postulates that after the Lockerbie disaster in 1988 and the search for 239 bodies, over forty police officers needed treatment for post traumatic stress disorder (PTSD) whereas among the soldiers involved (who on the whole were younger and less experienced) fewer had problems.[7] He suggests that this was possibly because the army, especially through its chaplains, had a machinery for the soldiers to talk through the horror.

On a smaller scale, when the fire brigade, who were much less involved than the police, returned to their headquarters, from the Akers Way incident, their official chaplain was there to meet them, presumably, to give them time to talk the matter through. No such ministry was immediately available to any others involved.

Rev Frank W. Parkinson, Air Force chaplain at the time, states that after the Gander air crash of December 1985 in which 256 US airborne troops were killed and there were no survivors, the debriefing of those involved took six months, presumably because of the numbers, not necessarily because of the depth and extent of the stress.[8]

Certainly chaplains in wartime have played crucial roles far beyond their brief of promoting the spiritual wellbeing of service personnel. The cynic (and maybe the pacifist as well) might suggest their role is merely to prop up a war machine. However, if 'identification' is part of the ordained and lay ministry and the chaplain is seen, in some sense, as God's representative in a community he or she will have various roles e.g. pastor, priest, prophet, counsellor and, in situations such as these, one who is able to reflect back to people involved, some sense of meaning and purpose to the event and its aftermath.

In an important article in *Psychiatry Today* in August 1991 Stuart W. Turner, senior clinical lecturer in psychiatry at the Middlesex Hospital, London, described post traumatic stress disorder in a number of helpful ways.[9] He gives five useful learning points:-

1. PTSD is a common reaction of normal individuals to extreme trauma.
2. Explanation and diagnosis are often reassuring.
3. It is important to treat any co-morbid conditions if they are present. For example, anxiety, phobias and depression may coexist in a person suffering from PTSD.
4. Successful psychological treatment is usually based on rehearsal of the trauma story.

5.   Prior planning in the training and availability of personnel who can help groups of people, as well as individuals, to come to terms with the event(s) is seen as vital.

There are, of course, differences between defusing, debriefing, specific Christian ministry and counselling though in fact they do overlap and are often confused with each other. For example, a Christian prayer counsellor might help a person to defuse past personal history as well as gently guiding into ways of coping and overcoming problems in the future.

The emergency services and the armed forces may well have excellent plans in this respect, but there remains a large number of individuals – bystanders, neighbours, and, in the case of Akers Way, children, who were witnesses, as well as teachers at the schools involved, for whom such prior planning is virtually impossible. Obviously in many cases there can be *no* prior training but Turner does make the point that perhaps the most exciting developments in the management of PTSD are in the early use of meetings of groups of survivors, encouraging individuals to talk about what has happened and facilitating early processing behaviour. Critical incident debriefing is of particular value following localised events and has been used after armed robberies and terrorist incidents in military units. Within one or two days of the event, a meeting is held to which individuals are invited. Basic ground rules concerning toleration of silence and confidentiality are agreed. The events are explored in group discussion, probably helping both to facilitate processing and to set the distress reaction within the normal range. By seeing that other individuals are also affected, it is easier to talk about what has happened and to resolve the traumatic impact.

Training for this technique is essential and it is now believed to be the best practice to use familiar management personnel as part of the normal work routine, rather than bringing in experts from outside the organisation. Although debriefing techniques are very helpful in the early stages, unfortunately there is little evidence to date that there is any significant reduction in symptoms of PTSD over the next few years. Joint planning teams with local authority and volunteer groups have been advocated but, in general, too much of the planning takes place after the event and serves to inhibit the early use of resources in the most appropriate way. Ministry in its wider sense to the traumatised is not just something specifically Christian but, nevertheless, there are at least five aspects which may overlap with medical care, but in some cases will be very different.

First, there is the need to open up the channels to give vent to feelings rather than push them down. Second, there is the matter of identification with someone else who is suffering. In Christian ministry there must eventually be a meeting at the cross of Christ and His pain and trauma. This is especially true in the case of anger, both individual and corporate. For the Christian this will sometimes entail the rather surprising notion of 'shaking your fist at God'. Authority figures will often be blamed, whether responsible or not, and those in the immediate family may be subject to irrational responses from the traumatised.

In learning to shake a fist at God the traumatised person of faith may discover that this in no way diminishes this love. This ability to release emotions towards God may, in a strange way, save those who are emotionally close to the person from physical and mental attack. Evidence for this is hard to deduce but examples of anger expressed Godwards is often found in the Psalms, e.g. Psalm 43. Jesus's cry of dereliction on the cross, 'My God, my God, why have you forsaken me?', can also come under this category. A passive submission to the will of God may well be appropriate for many but the more we discover about anger the better we find it must be for it to be expressed Godwards.

This sounds easier said than done and many will accept this as doctrinally and biblically true while finding the emotional identification much harder to practise. Much is rightly made of Christ's understanding of human pain and loss. (1 Pet. 2:21–4) and indeed there are five discernible elements in this.

Christ is the supreme example of innocent suffering.
Christ identifies himself with the sufferer.
Christ cares about the sufferer.
Suffering is a refining process ('vale of soul making', faith proving, 1 Pet. 1:7).
Justification of God's Spirit resting on the believer (1 Pet. 4:14).

Sheila Cassidy, writing in relation to the apocryphal book of Widsom 3: 1–6, quotes:

'But the souls of the virtuous are in the hands of God, no torment shall ever touch them.' In the eyes of the unwise, they did appear to die, their going looked like disaster, their leaving us, like annihilation; but they are in peace. If they experienced punishment as men see it, their hope was rich with immortality; slight was their affliction, great will their blessings be. God has put them to the test and proved them worthy to be with him; he has tested them like gold in a furnace, and accepted them as a holocaust.[10]

Has God really put them to the test? That is the question. How can we know? Do we believe in an intervening God, in a God who actively causes this person to have cancer or that person's child to die in a road accident? I really do not know what I believe, but the question no longer vexes me. I am quite content to remain in a state of unknowing.

What is clear, however, is that many people are purified by suffering. I have seen it in my own life and I meet it in the people around me. The mystery, of course, is that some people are warped and embittered by suffering while others are strengthened and become more loving and selfless. I believe that an important part of the vocation of the carer is to support people during a period of trial so that they may indeed grow and transcend the bonds of their captivity. When I write about spiritual growth of this sort, I sometimes take a sideways look at myself and wonder if I am imagining it: talking pious language to comfort myself and others. I was fascinated, therefore, when a nurse with whom I work, commented, 'It's really such a privilege to do this work, to be with these people. The way they grow – it's fantastic.'

Thirdly, and much related to the following aspects, is the exploration of the individual's relationship to God. It may be there is need to discover His love before much else can be accomplished. If the images of God in the traumatised person are weak, non-existent or distorted, then much of the specific Christian ministry might fall on stony ground.

The fourth element is the matter of prayer, anointing, laying on of hands and other physical acts of assurance. These may be ritual in the formal or informal sense, or they may just be a desire for human touch. One of the major growth areas in God's Church is the expression of physical feelings. Stemming perhaps from the Church of South India in 1947 the 'peace' is often a real endorsement of Christian love. It is frequently expressed in a way which would have surprised our Victorian Christian forefathers. The charismatic movement has in many ways taken this further so that traumatised individuals can be made to feel loved and supported and empowered to face life again.

Lastly, there is a cluster of experiences, such as healing of the memories, knowing and expressing forgiveness, release of bitterness, positive direction of anger, etc. The Holy Spirit is the Spirit of peace and so Christian ministry is much more rounded than many secular models of care. Christian ministry in this respect is often seen to be well-meaning but clumsy. Christian healing is not meant to be playing at being an amateur psychiatrist, but offering something very different. The rise in the number of healing centres and communities in recent years and the increase in healing services show the need, not just amongst Christians, but among others on the fringe of God's Church, to receive a spirit of well-being, of real 'shalom'.

It must be the mark of extreme secularisation in our society that 'no go' areas are being established. Clergy may well be stretched in their priorities; the welcome for their ministry may, at best, be a muted one; their personality, training and gifts may be better used in other directions; but these limiting factors do not imply that restrictions should be placed on Christian mission.

For my own part, following the Akers Way accident, my wife and I did suffer some after-effects in terms of sleepless nights. There was still the business of leading a medium-sized congregation in a large parish (I took two weddings only eighteen hours after the crash). There were sermons to prepare, people to see, meetings to attend, but the fact that I was able to share my feelings a little and small acts of kindness, such as cards and money in an envelope put through the door given specifically towards a meal out with my wife, indeed helped.

The chief police officer involved also suffered some symptoms of distress in the form of sleep disturbance but she, and others involved, did have resources for gradual debriefing, some of which were used in the weeks and months following the accident. (See Appendix C.) My interview with the assistant hospital chaplain involved shows a well-organised support system. (See Appendix B.)

I also interviewed the chief social services officer involved (see Appendix D) but his experience was, in the main, limited to preparing for the possible effects of the Gulf War. Planning for the after-effects of this potential disaster was, at least in this area, highly organised but, in the end, was mercifully not really needed.

Post traumatic stress disorder has then, in the last few years, become a recognised syndrome which can affect ordinary people faced with acute severe distress. In the case of an accident it may affect survivors, relatives, caring agencies and many others directly involved. It may also, though to a lesser degree, affect others who hear or read about the disaster, or as perhaps in the case of the Bradford FC disaster, those seeing it as it happens on TV.

Stuart Turner points out that PTSD is in fact a new name for an old disorder. In 1667 *five* months after the fire of London, Pepys described in his diaries, 'it is strange to think how, to this very day, I cannot sleep anight till almost two in the morning through thoughts of the fire.' Whether Pepys knew it or not, few died in the inferno. Perhaps his feelings were more related to the acute loss of property since four-fifths of the capital was destroyed.

A further after-effect is a sense of increased arousal and hypervigilance. A very minor example of the latter is that, in the course of writing this book, our house was broken into (during our absence) for the second time in a year, and the third time in as many years. Our response (the following day) was to leave a light burning all night, something we did not do before, and have not done since.

What then does the term PTSD mean and how does it differ from normal stress reactions? In the American Civil War the disorder was misleadingly called 'shell shock' and it was, of course, eventually recognised as a major distress factor in the First World War. Most people will experience some immediate stress symptoms after a serious incident. Fear is the usual response to danger, and depression is the response to loss and bereavement. Both of these can occur together after a traumatic experience involving threat to and loss of life. Normal feelings can include fear of a similar event occurring again, fear of breaking down, anger, helplessness, shame and anxiety, poor sleep and panic attacks; the fear response includes many physical symptoms such as dizziness, palpitations, aches and pains. After severe stress the individual is often more accident prone. Usually these symptoms settle down with sympathetic listening and the passage of time, without specific treatment.

The typical post traumatic stress disorder is a more intense, more persistent and often delayed reaction to a stressful incident. Usually the event is overwhelming and very intense, for example, serious fires, road traffic accidents, violence, sexual assaults, and wartime experiences. According to an authoritative psychiatry textbook by Gelder, Gath and Mayou, PTSD has three groups of features. The first is a mixture of anxiety symptoms similar to those described above. The second is persistent denial and avoidance of reminders of the event, with repeated vivid intrusive daytime flashbacks and recurrent distressing dreams of the event. Some patients experience a third group of features including an abnormal feeling of detachment, numbing or absence of normal emotions and loss of interest in everyday activities. Anxiety and depression increase in severity with flashbacks and reminders of the event and sometimes there can be bouts of aggression or excessive use of alcohol and drugs, damaging relationships at home and at work. PTSD may be a continuation of the initial response to stress or, in some instances, it may be delayed, occurring after an interval of a few weeks or days. Although the disorder usually resolves in a few months it can persist for many years in some cases.

Anyone can, of course, be affected by stressful events – survivors, victims, families, trained professionals, untrained helpers and bystanders. Not everyone is affected, as people differ so much in their family backgrounds, life experiences and personalities. There are also major differences in training and access to support in different professions and different parts of the country. Some people are very lonely and isolated while others have strong supportive networks of friends and relatives or belong to a strong Christian community. It hardly needs to be added that the strength of community bonding does not in every case have to be specifically Christian. However since the vast majority of images which the New Testament uses are heavily pluralistic in tone, e.g. 'household', 'body' etc., the exception being 'the bride of Christ', the local church of God *should* have a loving dynamic which can enfold the traumatised as well as any needy or lonely person. In recent years the growth in many churches of both formal and informal pastoral groups underlines both the need and the Christian response in this area.

Most professionals cope well much of the time and are able to carry out their duties efficiently throughout all sorts of disasters but prior training and planning is of great importance. However, it is possible that they may also have to develop strong mechanisms of repression and denial in order to cope with repeated traumatic incidents. Emergency care workers also require support and attention to prevent burn-out and other adverse reactions. Regular sleep and off-duty periods are vital and, as we have seen, some professionals have access to a trauma debriefing service after major incidents.

Helpers and bystanders often experience disturbed emotions and flashbacks. Sorrow and grief can be particularly intense when children are involved. However, the experience need not be totally negative and after the event is over some people do discover a heightened sense of the value and the precious nature of life itself.

If the stress is due to a recent event, all the help that may be needed is a chance to recall the unpleasant events and express the feelings associated with it to an understanding and reassuring person. Allowing these feelings to come out, and crying, gives relief and does not lead to loss of control. Conversely, stopping the expression of these feelings may lead to nervous and physical problems. It is important for the sufferer to have plenty of rest and sleep and make time to be close to family and friends. The aim is to try and keep life as normal as possible, but care should be taken to avoid accidents during this vulnerable period. Professional help should be sought from the family doctor in the first instance if symptoms are too intense to handle or if they are very persistent.

The medical treatment of PTSD attempts in the main to deal with the symptoms which are presenting and is tailored to the needs of the individual. Early intervention is important. A few doses of an anxiety-relieving drug to restore a normal sleep pattern may be required in the first few days. Sometimes the stressful events have to be talked about many times before the symptoms disappear. In such cases counselling by a skilled carer may be arranged. When the disorder is long-standing, it is harder to treat and often requires specialist help with the opportunity to receive further counselling techniques, grief work, social interventions, medication and treatment of any associated problems including anxiety and depression.

Does everyone have a breaking-point? It would appear so! For some it will, of course, be dependent on past experience, as well as present stress levels, etc. However, we may discern some hints of PTSD in the disciples following the crucifixion of Jesus e.g. distress in John 20:13 (Mary at the tomb); a desire for normality in John 21:3 (Peter returning to fishing), although that may be reading into the texts what is not really recorded!

For the Christian who might wish to view the Gospels from this angle, Jesus was a person who was stressed to a point far beyond that endured by any human being. 'My soul is overwhelmed with sorrow to the point of death' was His response in Gethsemane (Matt. 26:38). The seven last words from the cross bear the hallmarks of traumatic stress. This was not just a martyr going to his death, as so many of his followers have done since, nor was it a brave though foolish example. Jesus was bearing the sin of the world (1 Pet. 2:24). He was stressed beyond all human imagining by the sin of the world, and yet there does not seem to be the kind of 'brokenness' we might in ourselves experience in such a situation. Yes, His body was broken, His Spirit surrendered to God but did He exhibit the behaviour problems you and I might in such circumstances? The answer is indeed 'yes' and 'no'. Yes, because He was completely human and no, because He was (and is) the divine Son of God. The simple and, I believe, fundamental biblical approach of seeing Jesus as the sin-bearer of the whole world, including our 'dis-ease', is the heart of the good news of the gospel.

The only time the parents of the Akers Way incident were able to meet together was before and after the inquest and regrettably their therapy was not really helped by the atmosphere of the Coroner's Court. At least one person said that they felt they were on trial, such was the unsympathetic mood of the courtroom. My own limited experience of such proceedings confirms that forensic demands take little account of human needs.

Since the accident almost all the victims' parents and some of their other immediate family have sought medical help for reasons which may or may not be related to their loss. As a point of Christian sensitivity I have not enquired too deeply in this area, though on meeting the relatives either casually or at their homes, such information has been offered. Not all the parents were fit, healthy people before the accident, so the event may simply have exacerbated an already existing malady.

Stephen Homewood (who was the assistant purser on the *Herald of Free Enterprise* which capsized on the night of 6 March, 1987, with the loss of 193 lives) says, 'Zeebrugge certainly haunted me and still does but . . . with skilled help I have conquered the worst part of it.'[11] For all that, he describes graphically, how near 'breakdown' point he came and how eventually left the shipping company (with whom he had worked for over thirteen years) after being declared medically unfit. Part of the Carlton TV series in March 1994 *The Day I Nearly Died* related to this disaster. A couple in that programme stated how they had separated for a time following the trauma of that night but were now reunited with a stronger and more meaningful relationship.

In the final chapter of his book Stephen Homewood says he believes, 'there is now the professional talent to put together a pool of help ready to be called on in the event of another disaster . . . or rather in the aftermath'. Significantly his list of people trained in post-disaster trauma treatment does not include clergy. Among his hopes is the organisation, either by a voluntary body or through Government initiatives, of a 'Disaster Aftermath Unit'. At the time of writing, some years after Zeebrugge, sadly there does not seem much evidence of it being formed.

So the Christian gospel is the paramount attempt to provide meaning out of chaos. That it seems sometimes to fail is not, of course, because the message is faulty, but because its practitioners and agents either have not grasped it fully themselves, or are unskilled in putting it across, or simply because those on the receiving end are blind to its implications. This blindness may be demonically engendered (2 Cor. 4:4) or may be result of human sin and weakness. The reason why our society is not continually haunted by chaos can largely be attributed to its Christianised foundations. However, chaos still lurks at the gates. If people's moral insights become blurred, if powerlessness and fatalism begin to take over, then a paralysis may ensue. Rather like an animal transfixed with fear before the attacker pounces, so society can be frozen in a moral vacuum, neither able to progress to the future nor regress to a point in history when moral standards were deemed to be higher.

Letting go

However, there is also a parallel dimension to such care, i.e. the element of experiencing release and freedom in the 'letting go' of loved ones. Although perhaps not directly relevant, the request by the risen Jesus to Mary Magdalene at the dawn of the first Easter Day, can often be helpful. 'Do not cling [or hold on] to me' (John 20:17). Often there is all too much evidence of clinging on to a loved one which can be unwise, and both spiritually and mentally unhelpful: excessive visits to a grave or crematorium; keeping the vacant room exactly as it was at the time of death; retaining clothes; filling rooms with pictures, etc. Although much of the morbidity of mourning of a century ago has faded, the popularity of, say, Henry Scott Holland's poem which states that 'death is nothing at all' challenges the willingness of 'letting go'. It is the tension between holding a lively, wholesome memory of someone who has died and the commending of them to God's grace and mercy, which is at the heart of Christian care. It is a process which will develop in different ways, according to the individual, and the process will certainly take time but, if while that is happening a measure of progress can be seen, that surely is a sign of growing spiritual maturity.

It is evident that a person's own 'well-being' (and perhaps also 'being well') is surely part of this letting go. Perhaps we need more spiritual thermometer readings in the lives of Christians, and particularly bereaved Christians, to be able to measure not only progress towards wholeness, but also to recognise the point (or points) when there can be a contribution made to support those who follow along a similar path.

Access to God's love in an increasingly secularised society must seem, in some ways, more and more limited. If one of the main channels of His love i.e. the Church, is itself compromised by secularisation, then vast numbers of people will miss hearing the wonder of that love whether they are in a traumatised situation or not.

7

Finding God in a crisis

The title of this book *Where Was God last Friday?* must lead to other questions which, in some sense, are difficult or impossible to answer; or for which answers are only provisional. The old cliché about there being no atheists in a shipwreck may have some truth in it, but in cases of instant and sudden death we can have little idea of what thoughts pass through a person's mind. If that person is very young or, say senile, then ability to think rationally is almost non-existent. The predominant desire to escape must, inevitably, be the overwhelming human urge.

Stephen Homewood, quoted earlier[11] wrote, 'I am not religious and I did not pray or ask God for help on that night *or since*. I have no respect for religion, and I found some of the services and the hymns extremely comforting.' (my italics) That may be so but he also writes that he is a changed person: 'the night of 6th March 1987 has made me aware as I was not before, that our surroundings are beautiful and that we should help keep them so.' Not the encounter with a living God which is the biblical claim on our lives but certainly an opening of eyes about the precious nature of life itself. As a Christian minister I wonder about two aspects of Stephen Homewood's experience. Firstly, was there no one who would gently introduce him (and others) to the love of God in Christ? Secondly, had the accident happened in a different, less secular age, would he have put things differently instead of a simple (though very profound) awakening to the wonders of what he refers to as 'spaceship earth'?

For the Christian experiencing the aftermath of such trauma there should be more than the enhanced appreciation of the wonder of God's creation.

But what did the 20,000 victims of Pompeii in AD 79 or the 16,000 victims of Krakatoa in 1883, or the 50,000 killed in Peru in 1970 or the 140,000 killed at Hiroshima in 1945, think at the moment of chaos and death? In October 1966 after the tidal wave of black sludge wiped out two-thirds of the pupils of Aberfan village junior school the local evangelical pastor said, 'My faith has been shaken to the core. I don't know how I shall preach again'. I have no way of telling whether he was able to resume his active ministry, yet surely the grace and mercy of God is such that there are few situations where there is not recovery and a fuller and more mature ministry is discovered and enjoyed. Add to that every victim of war and sudden death, including the 5,000 who die on British roads each year, and a similar number who die in domestic and industrial accidents, and we can begin to see how immense the problem is. Nevertheless some answers can be postulated.

First, *the Christian understanding of God is a God not immune to suffering.* The cross of Jesus Christ, which is often anaesthetised or sanitized, is the most powerful and sharp reminder, not just of the love and judgement of God, but that pain, suffering and heartache are indeed at the centre of the Godhead. No wonder then that the idea of a mysterious, suffering servant of Isaiah has been a powerful notion in both Christian and Jewish theology.

Keith Ward has written: 'The classical conception of an impassive God, is totally inadequate as the interpretation of perfection. If love is a perfection, then a form of suffering – with greatness – must be an essential moment of divine life.'[12]

Of course there have been those who have made a very different response. Thus Bertrand Russell could claim early in this century that atheism was the only rational response to suffering. But for the most part suffering is not rational. The cry of the human heart in such events is not a cry for proof or philosophical reasoning but to know if God does exist and, if so, does He really care? Does His silence at such times mean His indifference? If, of course, it can be proved that He does not care, then surely only callous indifference is all that is left.

Jurgen Moltmann, who suffered considerably at the hands of the Nazis in the Second World War, has written extensively on this theme.[13] His stance is epitomised by his comments on Jesus in the Garden of Gethsemane in Mark's Gospel, 'Father, all things are possible; remove this cup from me.' It sounds, says Moltmann, like a demand; which is, in some way, softened in the accounts of Luke and Matthew with the words, '*If* it be possible'. Does the Father hear and reject His Son's prayer? It would seem so. There is, of course, a whole new cul-de-sac which can be unwittingly entered into here, namely that of Jesus' seemingly unanswered prayer. Elsewhere, Moltmann reminds us Jesus had claimed that He and the Father were One (John 14:10). Can it really be true that God does not respond to Jesus in His moment of deepest crisis? If God were impassive and remote then this response would be quite understandable but – his experience of being God's Son obviously led Jesus to teach and proclaim a facet of God as Father which had lain dormant in Jewish thinking.

Moltmann argues elsewhere that 'Christ had to learn obedience through the prayer which God rejected'.[14] But did God reject Jesus's prayer, especially in His great time of need? There have, of course, been – millions of people with poorer relationships to God than Jesus who have cried out to God and claimed that He was not there. A simplistic answer is that God did not reject Jesus, although he did reject him when he hung on the cross itself, but the answer was to be found in the realisation of God's will for His life, i.e. 'Nevertheless not my will but yours be done'. The answer seems to come obliquely rather than by direct revelation. Jesus was to discover, as many of His followers have done so since, that the answer lies (at least on this occasion) within Himself.

Jesus was, of course, going to cry from the cross, 'My God, my God, why have you forsaken me?' (Mark 15:34) and the seemingly unanswered prayer of Gethsemane can be seen as a foretaste of that incredible event. Moltmann goes on to state, 'Yet we, ourselves, cannot get used to the fact that this cry of the forsaken Christ stands at the centre of the Christian faith'.

Jesus's repeated use of the word 'why' is, of course, a point of identification with millions of others who have uttered the same cry. But that would seem a rather facile point to make. 'It is surely not by chance, either', says Moltmann, 'that this cry is the only time Christ does not call God familiarly "my Father" but addresses Him out of the infinite remoteness of separation as 'my God'.

Perhaps only those who come from a real experience of God as Father are best equipped to face up to unjustified suffering, or times when God seems silent, aloof or remote. Speaking of the dereliction Christ encountered, Moltmann concludes, 'With profound insight, Paul interpreted this as meaning from Gethsemane to Golgotha, Christ suffered God's judgment . . . "For our sake He made Him to be sin", 2 Cor. 5:21, and "He became a curse for us", Gal. 3:13.' For the Christian it is indeed Christ who suffers both with us and for us: Christ our brother in anxiety and fear; Christ our representative in time of need.

For believers there is no need to look further than the experiences spelt out in Isaiah 40 which begins, 'Comfort, comfort my people, says your God. Speak tenderly to Jerusalem, and proclaim to her that her hard service has been completed, that her sin has been paid for that she has received from the Lord's hand double for all her sins.' Here are words spoken to people at a time of deepest need. Faced by the Babylonian hordes, with war, starvation and exile becoming the everyday lot of thousands, a message is posted loud and clear, not about the logical or philosophical arguments about God's existence but about His tender, loving care.

Yet, suffering may not be directly as the result of spiritual disobedience as in the case of Israel two and a half millennia ago but, whatever the cause of the suffering, the character of God's love does not change.

Like Moltmann, it is often those Christians who have suffered most who can adequately expound how God can suffer in us. Often as not it is those who speak from a Catholic or Orthodox theological standpoint who seem to understand best. Sheila Cassidy in *Good Friday People* has a stunning quote from Elie Wiesel's chilling novel entitled *Night*. It describes the execution of two men and a young boy suspected of involvement in the sabotage of a power station.

One day when we came back from work, we saw three gallows rearing up in the assembly place, three black crows. Roll call. SS all around us, machine guns trained; the traditional ceremony. Three victims in chains – and one of them, the little servant, the sad-eyed angel.

The SS seemed more preoccupied, more disturbed than usual. To hang a young boy in front of thousands of spectators was no light matter. The head of the camp read the verdict. All eyes were on the child. He was lividly pale, almost calm, biting his lips. The gallows threw its shadow over him.

This time the Lagerkapo refused to act as executioner. Three SS replaced him.

The three victims mounted together on to the chairs.

The three necks were placed at the same moment within the nooses.

'Long live liberty!' cried the two adults.

But the child was silent.

'Where is God? Where is He?' someone behind me asked.

At a sign from the head of the camp, the three chairs tipped over.

Total silence throughout the camp. On the horizon, the sun was setting.

'Bare your heads!' yelled the head of the camp. His voice was raucous. We were weeping.

'Cover your head!'

Then the march past began. The two adults were no longer alive. Their tongues hung swollen, blue-tinged. But the third rope was still moving; being so light, the child was still alive . . .

For more than half an hour he stayed there, struggling between life and death, dying in slow agony under our eyes. And we had to look him full in the face. He was still alive when I passed in front of him. He tongue was still red, his eyes were not yet glazed.

Behind me, I heard the same man asking:

'Where is God now?'

And I heard a voice within me answer him:

'Where is He? Here He is – He is hanging on this gallows . . .'

Is that what gives meaning to suffering? Is it because God is in it, in it with us, that the obscene becomes transformed into the holy? I don't know, but I believe it is.[15]

It follows then that Christ's followers are not immune to pain and suffering. Jesus's prophecy, 'In the world you will have tribulation' (John 16:33) has been and is constantly being fulfilled. However, the Church itself has often been the persecutor as well as the persecuted, witness the worst aspects of the Reformation and the Counter–Reformation! In our own day and age there are plenty of examples of either self-destruction or situations where believers have inflicted pain on other Christians for the sake of tradition, pride or dogma, etc.

Second, *God is ultimately involved in all suffering*. There is the teaching, more apparent in the Old Testament than in the New, that evil is God's responsibility, primarily as a result of His judgement on a sinful world. The book of Revelation is, of course, full of such judgement on the wicked, and many thinking people hold this view. It is the question of undeserved suffering that perplexes both the believer and unbeliever alike. It remains an unanswered question, 'Why does God allow undeserved evil?'. The book of Job may have been written to answer such a question.

Usually there is a four-step statement regarding the problem of evil:

(i)   If God is all-powerful God could prevent evil.
(ii)   If God is all-good God would want to prevent evil.
(iii)   Evil exists.
(iv)   Therefore God is not all-powerful or all-good.

One way of developing this argument would be to say evil can be seen because we see its effects; we know that it exists. We know also that goodness exists, but where does God fit into what can be observed and, if He exists, which side is He on?

But none of the above deals with the problem of evil itself. Christian theology has attempted two ways of rationalising the problem.

First, there is the Augustinian approach which is essentially a biblical viewpoint hinging on the idea of the Fall which, in turn, brought about chaos in nature and human life, The Devil as a fallen angel is active and powerful in creating chaos. Sinful human beings can be so corrupted that they can be seen as evil, e.g. Hitler.

The second approach, as we shall see later, was adopted by Hick following Ireneus and hinges upon the creation of human beings through an evolutionary process, i.e. immature creatures living in a challenging and changing world. Although some articles have been written, there does not seem to have been a major book on the subject since John Hick's *Evil and the God of Love* published in 1968.[16]

The problem then can be looked at, and to some degree answered, in four ways:

1. *Victimisation*. Certainly every human being is subject to some form of injustice whether to a greater or lesser degree; it may be an institutionalised form, e.g. apartheid, or a judicial or commercial form, or simply being denied 'rights' which by any civilised standard are seen as fair and just. It is a well-worn, and more than partly true, argument to say that God is on the side of the weak and not the powerful, and this, of course is the main plank in the case of liberation theology, but it only goes some way to resolving the question.

2. *Lessons learned with hindsight*. It is only by continuous experiment that we learn from the mistakes of the past e.g. such mistakes as building in the path of a volcano, or inadequate structures in an earthquake zone. Sometimes the lesson has to be learned over and over again. To know what is preventable is both a prophetic and practical task that individuals as well as nations are slow to learn. In the case of the Akers Way crash the seat in question had, I believe, been on the site long before the road was improved and widened. For all that, a modern design would not have saved the lives of five young people; it is simply that no one seems to have thought about its position adjacent to the road.

Hindsight also plays a part in the sense that any suffering is not wholly negative and it is, indeed, in the words of Hick 'soul making'.

Charles Colson in *Who Speaks for God*'[17] points to a reductionist argument in the American best-seller *When Bad Things Happen to Good People* by Rabbi Harold Kushner. In it the author argues that God is indeed all-loving but not all-powerful. This seemingly easy answer which Colson rejects as unbiblical has, he claims, been accepted uncritically by many Christians simply on the grounds of providing *an* answer to an age-old question.

Not that Kushner writes out of personal ignorance (his own son died at 14) but providing such an answer would circumscribe the real problem. For Orthodox Christians the resurrection of Christ can and should be a powerful refutation of such arguments. On a personal level, though my experience is limited, I have heard little of Kushner's argument within the British Church scene. However, Kushner seems to put in point what many people are 'happy' to accept. Yes, God may be all-loving (and it is certainly nicer to think of Him that way), but His power is limited. The incarnation of Christ does show some aspects of a self-limiting God. His was choice freely made for the purpose of salvation history but it is very different from saying that God is ineffectual by nature! God's weakness on the cross should not lead us to conclude that Jesus's death could not have been prevented. No wonder Colson is surprised and not a little annoyed that so many Christians have accepted the rabbi's premise.

For all that the rabbi's book may not have actually crossed to Britain. It is the unconscious theology of western society that yes, God may exist, yes, He may love us, but He is limited and largely ineffectual. Yes, there may be many who would claim to be born again (like Charles Colson) and who would give powerful evidence to the converting work of the Holy Spirit in individual lives but He does not seem to intervene in the way many demand, and would wish Him to – or does He?

3. *The residual element of mystery*. There is in the end, faced with events for which no human being appears responsible either by design or negligence, the tendency simply to be agnostic in the face of those questions about suffering to which there seems no answer. It can be said that God is mystery and, in one sense, unknowable, but this does not help very much. On the other hand, if everything were explicable in human terms, we should be like God.

In man's search for discovery of more of the unknown, there is of course the sense of wonder summed up in the cliché, 'the more I know, the more I realise I don't know'. It is not just a theological question 'Why did it happen?', it is an endtime and pastoral question, and in a world where instantaneous answers are highly prized it is one which cannot ever be answered in that kind of way. Hick only partially attempts to unravel the level of mystery but concludes that the 'soul making' process does in fact fail as often as it succeeds.

4. *The cross of Christ.*

No attempt, however feeble, at answering the question 'Why does God allow unjust suffering?' can be arrived at without further reflection on why God's Son should suffer. Certainly there is an element of victimisation and of mystery. There is also an element of hindsight. Would the disciples have acted in the same way if the events were to happen again?

There is the power of forgiveness, the symbolism and the atonement that Christians down the years have seen in the innocent suffering of the Son of God. There is also the element of sacrifice in the cross of Christ. It is no wonder that in the First World War (fought largely by two countries that were in theory Christian in their ethos) 'crucifixion became the controlling image of those who thought themselves to be crucified'.[18] Christians, if they are to be of any effect, must live, as George Carey has said, 'on the dark side of the Cross' in order to enter into the darkness of people's lives. It also needs to be added that, in a society which either attempts to deny death or sees it as the worst thing to happen to a person, through the cross of Christ, death comes to be seen in a totally different light.

When Hegel received from his pupils on his sixtieth birthday a medal which showed an owl and a cross, Goethe reacted angrily: 'Who can demand I love the cross if I am forced to share its burden?' For him its harshness and nakedness was in conflict with the humane and rational. Hegel's reaction was different: 'An airy decorative cross is always a cheerful object'.

Down through history the idea of a God incapable of suffering keeps re-emerging, from Aristotle who put forward the notion of a God who cannot love, but can only be admired, to Dostoyevsky for whom man makes his own God which conveniently is incapable of suffering.

Perhaps, more than anything else, in what is sometimes called a post-Christian society, where forms of religion exist – or at least a variety of 'isms' in which degrees of faith and trusts are often exhibited although they seem to fail modern humankind at least in the western world: – the Christian faith does not postulate stoic acceptance of unjustified suffering or a cheap fatalism but something much more profound and, therefore, much harder for the secular mind to accept. Just as J.B. Philips wrote, speaking of British society immediately after the war and also its Church, 'Your God is too small'[19]. In spite of much implicit religion in Britain there are, perhaps, not the reserves of real Christian belief to enable individuals to cope in crises.

There must be few disasters where this residual belief does not rise to the surface or where more likely, the church in its pastoral care offers hope in a dark moment, but how deep or long-term the commitment will be is a matter for speculation. Certainly in a 'Decade of Evangelism' Christ's body cannot be content with offering spiritual 'first aid', no matter how good that might be.

Erik Peterson has said, 'The apostolic church, which is founded on the apostles who became martyrs, is always at the same time, the suffering church, the church of the martyrs.'[20] As an established religion, and in its bourgeois form, Christianity has become estranged from this truth.

It should not go unnoticed too that the Christian doctrine of hope has much to offer, not simply pious hope in eternal life, a concept which is largely lost on secular humanity, but hope allied to purpose, even though that is difficult to see at the time. It is not inappropriate here to add a personal note that, in 1972 when the emptiness of personal tragedy hit me very hard, one line in a letter stood out. It simply said, 'Extract every positive aspect from this painful experience, for that will stand you in good stead in the future.' The frail threads of the positive aspect of unjust suffering are not mere straws in the wind, but the material to weave a rich tapestry which, to those who dare respond, is both light in the darkness and also a multicoloured carpet into the heart of God Himself.

Good out of evil

If then we are left with some questions, which seem in this life to be unanswerable, what positive aspects remain? Shakespeare gives Henry V the words, 'There is some soul of goodness in things evil would that men observing would distil it out'.

For the Christian building the kingdom of God is, of course, an absolute priority. The catalogue of sheer human kindness, friendship, caring, etc., in even a relatively local disaster such as Akers Way, would take long to recount. It speaks volumes that the marks of Christianity are not totally erased in semi-secular British society. Other cultures may act differently, for example because of 'responsibility suits' in the USA people have indeed walked away from such accidents, and a law is now in force making this a criminal act. There may be the stance of passive indifference in the face of extreme suffering either because the suffering is so vast, or because traditional religious values have engendered indifference, or simply because there is not the means to help even if there were the will. Certainly being 'neighbour' to those in need was one of the most practical of Jesus's parables. In some ways it is the easiest to put into practice, in others, much harder.

Hick says,

It is true sometimes . . . no one can know how often or how seldom . . . there is sown or there comes to flower even in the direst calamity, graces of character that seem to make the calamity worthwhile e.g. a selfish spirit moved to compassion . . . a soft indulgent character made strong in the fires of adversity. But it may also fail to happen and instead of gain there may be sheer loss. Instead of enabling, affliction may crush the character and wrest from it whatever virtue it possessed.[16]

Sadly, Hick does not develop this any further. He seems content to leave the divisive nature of just and unjust suffering at that point without speculating as to what God's will might be or even tabulating some profit and loss account.

When considered mainly from a pastoral and not specifically theological stance, it seems that suffering opens a 'window of opportunity' that does not happen at other times. The bystander can show what it means to be a 'neighbour', the affected given a chance to think afresh (or in many cases for the very first time) about the meaning of life. The society in which we live has, on the whole, very superficial values. That is not to say that life is held cheaply, but there has been an erosion explosion in the whole field of morality, marriage and family life. The standards and values of some aspects of the media influence and even dictate the morals of the majority, and at best the moral standard is regarded only as what seems best for the common good (who decides what the common good is, is a question which always remains unanswered). In this kind of atmosphere any personal crisis is both a pastoral and an evangelistic opportunity. To put it another way, some may react by seeking to re-erect barriers which seem in a crisis to have been broken down; others may realise that there is more to life than the materialistic values engendered and encouraged by the western world.

Certainly, perhaps until the time of the Enlightenment, there was often resignation and acceptance. 'It was the will of God', said Katherine of Aragon after failing to produce a male heir to the throne and seeing five other children stillborn or die in infancy. Sadly, whilst rejecting that passive acceptance and perhaps fatalistic view, we have, it seems, little to put in its place.

Hick certainly rejects the idea that the world is in the grip of evil, a view which brings him in direct conflict with the New Testament (Rom. 8:22) and, more specifically, Psalm 53. He can only conclude, 'I do not now have an alternative theory to offer that would explain in any rational or ethical way why men suffer as they do. The only appeal is to mystery.'

It is, perhaps, then the role of the pastor, and I suggest, the evangelist, to attempt to unpack that mystery. Some of the attempts at this will be clumsy with inappropriate words and actions. However, Christian love must be the compelling motive. The emergency services will meet the immediate human needs and the requirements of the law. The statutory authorities may take action to see that, if possible, the disaster is not repeated. Security may be enhanced in the case of terrorist attacks, but it is the long-term felt needs that remain.

In the face of suffering the cruellest answer to the question 'Why?' is 'Why not?' In a previous parish an active Christian mother replied thus to her teenage son when he asked this question on hearing he had a life-threatening cancer, but she also asked, 'Who would you rather had it instead?' Is there a particular immunity given to Christians and others which affords them special protection from disease or accident? With the advance of medical science and the improvement in life-spans there has grown up a viewpoint which is death-denying and expectant of such immunity.

As has been suggested previously, only in the cross of Christ can any meaningful answer be found. Why did God allow His Son to suffer such a cruel and ignominious death? Charles Ohlrich says much about the theology after Hiroshima but concludes, 'Our journey will lead to the cross of Jesus Christ. There and only there will we find a satisfactory answer to the question of God's goodness in the light of human suffering.'[21]

Resurrection life!

Yes, central to the Christian gospel is the message of the cross. Yet it is an empty cross! Not just because its victim has long been taken down and reverently buried. Not because the mangled bloody body of Jesus was entombed in a rich man's vault. The cross is empty because of the resurrection.

Can then we ask whether the resurrection of Jesus has anything to say in situations of disaster, not least in the aftermath of a terrible local accident?

First, there is a resurrection motif to life itself: 'springtime' with its burst of new life and birth after a dark winter. Holidays, new clothes, nice surprises, healing, recovery from illness: all point to part of human life where things simply get better. God, it seems, has set this kind of scenario in the hearts of men and women. It falls woefully short of the Christian understanding of resurrection life but it is a significant pointer in this direction.

Second, there is simply the idea of change and growth. That the latter is dependent on the former cannot be doubted. The disciples were not the same people after they met Jesus for the first time, but that change pales in comparison to when they were confronted by the risen Jesus. Compare, if you will, the first meeting of Jesus with the fishermen by Lake Galilee (Mark 1) and their meeting after the resurrection (John 21). The same location – well almost – same people, same Jesus. The initial challenge is to follow Him and learn to catch other disciples, now they must also learn to disciple others for Christ. The backdrop to the first meeting was years of settled life with traditional habits and attitudes, but this way of life is interrupted by the call of Jesus. The second backdrop is of three years of semi-nomadic life following a wandering preacher/teacher, the trauma of Good Friday and Easter morning. So whether it is from a position of relative tranquillity or from one of great chaos, it is the same Jesus who confronts human beings with His claims.

We can often seek to escape into the events of our immediate past in order to avoid real discipleship. Sometimes, the trauma of a recent event can be so 'mind-blowing' and emotionally disturbing that the claims of Jesus go unheeded. Even when our backgrounds have been relatively settled, it can be life-threatening to follow Jesus.

So, in Christian terms, resurrection is more than a pious hope; it is more than getting back to normality after a time of traumatic upheaval; more than a feeling of 'life will get better'; more than the calm after a storm; more than optimism overriding pessimism: it is at its heart a meeting with a person!

In a materialistic and relativistic age the Church of Jesus needs to stand clear from the world. If you like, it needs to be confrontational and state what resurrection life is really like, not the substitute we so often adhere to. How inadequately the message has so often been conveyed. The parable of the weeds and seeds in Matthew 13 shows clearly how people respond, or do not respond, to the claims of Jesus. However, I know deep down that despite all the love and care I might show to others, I often do not put the claims of Jesus with brilliant clarity. Perhaps the 'evangelist' which is the birthright in every Christian, needs to be resurrected as well. For others, perhaps it is the 'pastor' that needs to rise again!

So resurrection life means an encounter with the risen Christ. It can never be an exercise to 'turn the clock back' nor a denial of past history or simply relief of guilt, but it must be a spiritual meeting which can be more life-changing than even the most painful, chaotic and traumatic event human beings ever have to face. Such is the claim of Christian resurrection life. It is a claim to which millions world-wide can testify. One example will suffice.

During the course of the writing of this book the parish was engaged in the search for a new curate. Among the enquirers was Clive Okill. He was due to come and look round the parish and the date was set for Friday 30 July, 1993. The previous

Sunday (St James' Day) gunmen burst into St James' Church, Capetown, where he had once served, and killed eleven people including his own nineteen-year-old son, David. It was then, of course, several weeks before we were able to meet. As is the way of things an appointment was not made. He was, however, invited to preach at St Mary's twice, and his sermons definitely came from the heart! Here was a minister needing love and care himself whilst, at the same time, being expected to give it to others. Be that as it may, what is crucial is his encounter with the resurrection life of Jesus.

And is God silent?

C.S. Lewis once said that pain and suffering were God's megaphone, God's loudspeaker, if you like his way of drawing our attention to Him. Dr George Truett, the great preacher from Dallas, Texas, used to say, 'Be careful how you suffer . . . When sorrow comes we are not to be bitter; we are to let it bring us closer to God.'

There is an obvious parallel in these two statements: they both advocate that pain, sadness and suffering are means by which we can draw closer to God. This seems contradictory to the nature of God, as we have always understood that the God of our past, whatever that past may be, is a God of love, a God of mercy and a God who shouldn't wish suffering on anyone. We feel that a God who allows catastrophe to befall a person, a family or a nation is not a God worth following, least of all worshipping. And we feel that, if we should feel the pain or in C.S. Lewis' case, if the megaphone be sounded, when we reached out in response to Him, we would find a stone wall of silence! This God does not make sense.

One of God's great men, the apostle Paul, knew a great deal of suffering. He was persecuted unmercifully for the sake of Christ. He experienced beatings, imprisonment, stoning, shipwrecks, mental, physical and spiritual torment, year after year. He lost his family, social status, authority and wealth. Yet he is one of the greatest examples of faith when he says: 'I have learned to be content whatever the circumstances' (Phil. 4:11).

Content! When a child is lost, a cancer diagnosed, an income gone, a partner unfaithful! Content! How? Why? For these questions there is no easy answer. There are many glib responses, but no real solutions to the searing pain that tears through body, soul and mind. Pills may bring sleep and dull the senses but they do not bring rest and they do not bring peace. Well-meaning quotations from Scripture have little impact. To have someone say, 'Well, at least we know that she is with the Lord in heaven' is lost because we do not want the individual to 'be with the Lord', *we want him (her) to be with us*! King David, after the death of his infant son got up from his grief, washed his face, and said, 'He cannot return to me but I will go to him . . .' (2 Sam. 12:23).

I suppose that an understanding that death is not final does help with the pain. It does not remove it; nothing removes the hurt. Pain and grief are very much a part of our humanity and we would be less than human if we did not feel as we do. Knowing that one day (Oh God! those words 'one day') every tear will be wiped away is seen not with the eye that suffers but with the eye of faith. A certain hope, a certain trust, a certain looking ahead holding on faithfully to the promise, however vague, that God will not abandon his children.

When hurt and despair come upon us we are faced with certain choices. We can choose to remain angry with God and follow the path of anguish, revenge and bitterness, a path which will certainly lead to more suffering, or we can choose to let God be God. It is a simple act of faith that says He has not lost control and he knows what is best. This path results in us saying, 'No, I don't understand and I don't know how all this will fit together or any of the reasons for it. In fact, I'm not even going to ask for an explanation. I've chosen to accept the fact that God is God and I am His creation, servant and, more important, His child.' Then we need to leave it there. If He is God and if He is who the Bible says He is, then He can't mess up. He just can't.

The panacea for pain is time. 'And it came to pass . . .' We cannot understand the mind of God: for now we see through a glass darkly. This planet is not heaven. And as long as we remain on earth there will be suffering because sin abounds. Clouds will continue to overshadow the human race, yet all the while the still small voice of God echoes through time. If we listen carefully we hear Him whispering to us. 'Call on me in the day of trouble and I will deliver you' (Ps. 50:15); 'I will never

leave you nor forsake you . . .' (Heb. 13:5); 'And as your days
so shall your strength be '(Deut. 33:25). God may not speak as
we would have him speak. While he may appear silent, he is
not absent.

Dr Robert Speer tells of an experience he had with his young
son. The boy and father were away from home and had to
sleep in a strange bed. In the middle of the night the little
boy awoke, frightened by the darkness. 'Daddy,' he cried out.
'Yes, son', answered the father. 'Are you there?' asked the
boy. 'Yes, son, I've been here all the time,' said the father.
'Even in the darkness?' asked the little boy. 'Yes, son, even
in the darkness.'

At times of grief (especially for those with little or no Christian
understanding as in the case of the Akers Way accident) the
intensity of the moment can shut the mind and heart to the tears
of others, as well as to God Himself. It is only those who really
know Christ to be raised who can begin to minister to others
in such circumstances? I have no evidence of this. However, I
do believe with a firm conviction that the resurrection of Jesus
does make a profound difference to the way in which death
and bereavement is faced and I know this now, not as biblical
doctrine, nor as sermon material, but as a real experience of
the living Lord.

8

Reporting in the media

Under this heading I want to give some personal reflections on my perception of the role of the media after the accident in Akers Way, during the trial a year later and at subsequent periods in between.

It cannot be denied that the media has an important role to play and, in a free society, it should not it be strictly controlled; more than a bare reporting of the facts is involved.

Air Vice-Marshal Brook, the Government's Emergency Planning Adviser, has warned that strict controls on the media will need to be imposed when the next incident of major proportions occurs:

> In little more than twelve hours after Pan Am 103 crashed, there were at least 500 media people in Lockerbie, including seventeen TV crews and a vast array of equipment. The police should make sure the media does not get in the way of the emergency services. With some organisations using helicopters, control of air space should be considered. The media may need to be reminded that in the period immediately following a disaster, no one can know precisely what has happened. Any statements should not include speculation on the cause of the disaster.[22]

Yet sadly the latter was all too true in the Akers Way tragedy. One headline proclaimed, 'Shattered estate's simmering anger as joyride tragedy haunts grieving families'. That quote was not published immediately following the accident but some twelve months later after the verdicts at Gloucester Crown Court. It distorted the truth on at least two counts. In the first instance, it gave the false impression that most, if not all the families in the area, were affected. In fact, the area involved can not strictly be defined as an 'estate', council or otherwise. Secondly, the drivers involved, although travelling at excessive speed, were not 'joyriding' in the contemporary usage of that word.

My own worst experience occurred on the morning of Monday 23 September, 1991, when on leaving the rectory to take the funerals of the two youngest victims, I was confronted by a TV news producer and his assistant almost demanding that a camera be put in the church to record or broadcast the service. His opening words on seeing my clerical attire were 'Talk of the devil' which were hardly polite or apt in the circumstances.

In fact, we did allow a land-line to be used by both local radio stations to record the service, but it was done with maximum discretion and consideration and, as far as I know, did not cause any offence. The local junior school choir came to sing at this particular service, but it was only by dint of considerable ingenuity that they were 'smuggled' in and out of the back entrance to the church well away from the media cameras.

There seem to be at least five areas where the media could (and need) to be involved: the reporting of the incident itself; investigating the effect on the community and its leaders (in this case also the local church); highlighting the plight of the victims; documenting the reaction by the emergency services; and discussing the political and social consequences.

Of all the groups of people affected it is the victims' families who in the Akers Way tragedy were most vulnerable to intrusion and sadly this will always be true. One or two families were fortunate to have a 'minder' in the person of a brother or male cousin who answered the door or telephone. Others were not so fortunate, and I heard many heartfelt cries about privacy being invaded with faces at windows and shouting through letter-boxes. Regrettably, many of the statements made in the heat of the moment, at the time of the accident, were reported a year later as contemporaneous responses. This arose because at the end of the trial the families, the police and myself agreed that only the police inspector would speak to the media. Consequently, the latter felt somewhat frustrated at being unable to speak to others involved who did not wish to prolong the period of anguish any longer. For my own part, my sabbatical leave had officially started a few days prior to the commencement of the trial and my telephone was diverted to my colleague who deftly fielded most of the questions by simply stating that I was on study leave when, in fact, I was attending the trial each day!

In this particular incident, the role of the police liaison officer cannot be understated. He, was in fact a civilian, but was a former chief inspector of the Wiltshire Constabulary. In this capacity he had no authority other than that of persuasion which worked quite well at the time of the funerals, but was less effective as the families left court after the trial.

Unfortunately, responsibility in the media is still a grey area in our society. In the matter of good investigative journalism and balanced reporting of the news, there is much that is worthwhile. Nevertheless, the invasion of privacy is often justified by the intense competition involved and this leads to distasteful reports and heightened distress for the victims' families. Some would question whether privacy as such is a Christian value but, surely, it can be argued from a Christian perspective that individuals under stress have particular rights that need to be respected. 'Public interest' is often quoted as the reason for sensational reporting, but who is to decide what 'public interest' really is, especially over and against private grief?

What is in the interest of the public is not necessarily in the public interest. The argument that certain individuals have rights when confronted by commercially-driven interests is not unimportant. Submissions by the Church of England Communications Unit in 1992[23] to the Calcutt review (self-regulation of the press), the National Heritage Committee enquiring into privacy and media intrusion, and the Private Member's Bill by Clive Soley MP into freedom and responsibility in the press, all make the point that the existing code of practice drawn up by the Press Complaints Commission (PCC) is not effective enough. They take this view not necessarily because it is a 'self-regulating' code but because it is largely unenforceable.

One paragraph from these submissions will suffice to sum up the Christian stance. For the Christian faith, with its belief that a person reflects the image of God, it is important that respect is accorded to the individual. This respect must include the right to privacy. In a situation where a person or their family is undergoing stress caused by personal tragedy, it is vital. Unwarranted instrusions into grief by the use of a telephoto lens or persistent telephone calls are deplorable. The pastoral needs of the individual should be paramount.

So, the biblical concept of justice is perhaps more relevant than the westernised notion of privacy. Certainly, the formulation of fair and workable legislation could be described as a 'super-human' task.

I am reliably informed that in Halsbury's *Laws of England* there is no general right to privacy. There is, however, legislation regarding nuisance, libel, and trespass, but frequently, in cases where the media have intruded, the violation is often of a temporary nature though of an intensity and volume which could not come at a worse time. National public figures might well experience such harassment but often they have courted publicity in the past to further their 'image'. It is difficult to consider their difficulties alongside those of ordinary people who find themselves thrust into the headlines through no action of their own.

On 30 September, 1992, after the verdict at Gloucester Crown Court was announced, and having agreed that no one other than the police inspector would speak to the press, the families and I were assailed en route to the nearby car park. On such an emotive occasion it was deeply distressing to have to run the gauntlet of the media, with microphones being thrust into people's faces for instant comment. The dignity and bearing of the families involved was commended by the prosecuting counsel during the trial, but that bearing must have been stretched to the limit at those times when the media overstepped the mark.

It is also worth noting that Clive Soley's 1993 Bill on this subject pointed out that most of the complaints against the press concerned the accuracy of the reporting and only 7–8 per cent regarded the intrusion of privacy. Nevertheless I understand the European Convention on Human Rights does have two clauses, 8 and 10, which protect press freedom *and* the interests of privacy.

Jesus and privacy

Jesus certainly valued the 'privacy' of being in the presence of His Heavenly Father. He sought solitude with God away from the demands of others (Matt. 14:23). He taught about the value of privacy in prayer (Matt. 6:6). The opportunity of being quiet and alone in the presence of God has been prized in most Christian traditions. 'Privacy' itself is not enshrined but it is seen as time set aside for a particular purpose. When the rights of individuals are set over and against public interest the key question is whether that interest is voyeuristic in nature and intrusive in practice. To find the answer, appeal needs to be made to other biblical concepts, and in the end, it is a matter of plain, natural justice.

The Calcutt report defined privacy as 'the right of the individual to be protected against intrusion in his personal life or affairs or those of his family, by direct physical means or by publication of information'. Sadly no bishop took part in the debate in the House of Lords in July 1992 though there were obvious moral issues at stake. Clearly some of those moral issues with regard to privacy are culturally bound. If an Englishman's home is his castle, why not a Scotsman's or a Western Samoan's? We need to be able to sift through cultural norms with regard to privacy in order to discern what is a Christian understanding, and not simply a western social norm.

Since the events of 13 September, 1991, and the subsequent trial I have been in correspondence with one of the TV journalists involved. Her personal stance is somewhat different from what is often seen in the tabloid press. She states that 'I hope my coverage of events reflected my overriding aim to remain objective and fair; to report the facts. Also by telling the news on a human level appears to help the viewers understand and empathise with the story.' Unsolicited, she added that the role of the Church was to work hard to deflect anger and bitterness in the community and serve as a focus for mixed-up emotions.

Finally she says, she 'would support legislation to protect the privacy of members of the public but not politicians or other people accountable to the public.' She adds that the person appointed by the police to liaise with the media is not always the right person to enforce such legislation; although it was largely effective in the Akers Way incident, it would have been wholly inappropriate at Hillsborough, for example.

Steven Homewood in *A Hero's Story* recalls a graphic incident where the press literally swooped on someone, so overcome with grief after the Zeebrugge disaster, that he sat on the floor of a hotel lobby convulsed and racked with tears. The press and TV demanded answers to their questions. One photographer lay on the floor and poked his camera through the man's arms to get a 'better' shot. The distraught survivor was oblivious to them all. However, it was a situation where anger could have exploded into violence. Human dignity was simply thrust aside because media interest demanded it. It is a situation which is repeated far too often when people are in a vulnerable state and unable to defend themselves.

Victims twice over

Victim Support has recently produced a brief report under the above title[24]. It highlights some twelve cases where victims of crime were subjected to either inaccurate or judgemental reporting, where the character of the victim is misrepresented. It is true that these case histories concerned victims of crime rather than those traumatised by accident; however, it is the view of a number of responsible observers that the latter often suffer just as badly from misrepresentation, and in some cases suffer worse.

In Sweden journalists have combined to produce a code of practice which appears more civilised than that which pertains *at times* in Britain.

When questioned by the media, people in a state of shock will often reveal information about themselves which afterwards they wish they had never divulged. The fact that these details may be irrelevant to the main story is largely ignored.

Much that has been written in recent years regarding individual privacy and the freedom of the press has been from a reactive stance or from a forensic angle. A response is now needed from a biblical and theological viewpoint. There will be many common strands with the views already published and certainly a recognition that we live in a very different age to that of the Bible. (Can you imagine the scene when Jesus is on the way to Calvary with the newshounds after Him?) Nevertheless, the task of biblical theology is to sift out the strands of Scripture which do apply to such situations. The Bible is the word of God; it is relevant to the whole of life and not just some sections of it.

Although the number of national newspapers has declined in recent years, the press, radio and TV have local, regional and national reporters. The intensity of competition is a very obvious phenomena which can also lead to accusations of unethical means to gain advantage over media rivals.

However, it is not only the victims of disasters and crimes who have cause to complain and who are often not in a position to respond in an effective way. The spouses and children of some of those who might well seek the limelight are also at risk. Public figures of course, often take it as the price of fame or notoriety, or the cost of being in the public eye. Even if such treatment from the media cannot be justified in terms of Christian morality and behaviour, most public figures expect some intrusion into their private lives. It could be argued that their families must and should have a greater right to protection.

One former cabinet minister's wife questions the absolute freedom the press seems to have acquired for itself: 'the furry, phallic boom of a film camera thrusting at us . . . out for gloat quotes and the grief snaps, those images of other people's troubles which give such tremendous pleasure and help raise the circulation figures of our estimable tabloid newspapers'. 'Substantial elements of the press are no longer protectors but savagers of the innocent'. 'I learnt from sympathetic and irate neighbours that a fluctuating flock of presspersons had spent the day doorstepping our block of flats greatly upsetting some elderly residents who felt it a gross invasion of their (and our) privacy.'[25]

Later on, at a different, rural location, she recalls, 'Sadly, we did not manage to protect our daughter (aged 8) from this. Having seen my tears after I was chased by journalists in a Westminster street . . . our daughter spent much of Saturday in tears herself, having been so scared by strange men staring at her through the leaded panes . . . Such pain should not be inflicted on the innocent.'

Clearly, it seems that self-regulation by the media breaks down on many occasions and is not working to help the innocent when they, of all people, should be protected. In theological terms the idea of self-regulation, either by individuals or by a community, is somewhat questionable. Self-regulation in the Bible derives either from obedience to the law or from God's Holy Spirit indwelling the life of the church and individual believers. It demands positive action, rather than the notion of doing as little as possible.

The code of practice drawn up by the Press Complaints Commission (PCC) is in some ways an admirable idea and is meant to cover such matters as inaccuracy, harassment, intrusion and discrimination by newspapers and magazines. It does not include TV and radio. Membership of the PCC is drawn from the public and the press; seven members are actually editors of national, regional or local newspapers and magazines. It can be argued from the outset that this body does not have sufficient independence to be truly objective. In any case in this matter 'prevention is better than cure' and at this point in time few ordinary people are willing to make use of the courts to right their grievances. The idea of the PCC, although admirable in many ways, seems something of a 'paper tiger', and perhaps its powers as well as its independence need to be strengthened. Even so little can be done to change the motives of the newshound in today's competitive environment. It could be changed. The Church of England Communication Unit's submission to the Calcutt Commission identifying the 'pastoral needs of the individual' does not sit easily with media appetite. It is a clash of interests which cannot be lightly resolved, especially when most of the power is weighted on one side.

In the matter of redress many people affected in this way feel, 'why bother?' The media come and go, their interest is transitory, they will pass on to other stories, and so on. That was certainly how I felt in September 1991 when I contacted the PCC to see how I could complain and received their booklet and literature. I 'failed' to take any further action, perhaps because I am not naturally a complaining type of person or, more likely, because other events preoccupied my time and mind.

The situation would be improved if an enlarged PCC were to be pro-active and scrutinised the media before the complaints arose. This, in my judgement, does not smack of 'thought police' but would tip the scales to balance out what often seems unjust and unfair treatment of many innocent people.

The age-old question as to whether the media report, reflect or mould public opinion can, I suspect, never be answered satisfactorily. What can be done is to ensure that the debate is continually kept open and that constant pressure is maintained upon the media to ensure its answerability to the public as a whole. This is essential if our society is to be just as well as free. One other result of the continued reports of media harassment and misreporting is that new guidelines are being issued to the police at a national level.

Certainly my own previous experience while vicar of Greenham, following the announcement that Cruise missiles would be coming to the local base in 1981, was an asset in learning to deal with the media, but, I have no training in that field, apart from remembering from college a statement to the effect 'Make friends with the local press'. Experience of broadcasting on local radio is also an asset but, there is a danger that if anyone is naive, vulnerable, or tempted to enjoy the limelight, then the work of God's church can be put at some disadvantage. Those Christians who see the media as worldly and perhaps, have minimal contact with it, could be accused of escapism, but surely they have a point when they highlight its excesses and abuses.

When ordinary people, through being the victims of crime or accident, are put in the public spotlight, the onus is on the media to demonstrate that they understand that the freedom they demand (which in a democracy should be widely supported) brings also with it responsibilities. Unfortunately it is the failure of the minority of irresponsible reporters which brings victims and the media into conflict.

9

The Importance of Ritual

'Ritual can unite, speculation can divide us', so wrote F.H. Keeling in 1916 during the middle of the First World War. It is an obvious generalisation, but even our secularised society has not replaced ritual. People still shake hands (or shake fists), put flowers on graves, stand in queues, say 'hello' to friends, and so on. Ritual is part of the warp and woof of life, although it might not be as stylised or formal as it once was. New rituals may evolve, such as protest marches or 'New Age' fashions.

In an industrialised nation ritual will not be related to the seasons and less stress may well be put on 'rites of passage', nevertheless there is still a desire in our society for ritual. Funeral directors will point out that the majority of people still chose a traditional burial or a cremation while only a small proportion desire a totally secularised approach.

Whilst Anthony Russell has written, 'In advanced societies religion has ceased to fulfil those integrating and regulating functions which it fulfilled in traditional society',[26] nevertheless when disaster strikes it is often the established religion (or in a few cases what is left of it) that provides most of the appropriate ritual. There are exceptions as we shall observe later, but it is worth noting that after the accident in September 1991 the major rituals, i.e. the funerals, were all Anglican, and all except one, took place at the church some 600 yards from the scene.

Alan Billings, in the account of his involvement with the Hillsborough disaster, points out that 'we live in a society which seeks to push away the reality of death on the one hand and which has progressively done away with ritual on the other. We have frowned on too much grief . . . don't upset yourself . . . don't become morbid . . . don't let yourself go. We have shortened the time of mourning to twenty minutes at the crematorium. We have forgotten to pray. We have locked up our churches.'[27] In these circumstances it is not surprising that people, especially young people, will devise their own rituals; witness the galaxy of scarves and hats surrounding the goal-posts at Hillsborough following the tragedy there.

Freud, who dismissed corporate ritual as simply institutionalizing individual 'hang ups', referred probably to churches or synagogues where daily acts express the need for some kind of worship. The thrust of this chapter is not about the normal but about the abnormal, and the need to make some corporate sense of it.

Roger Grainger says, 'The practice of corporate ritual is a function of being human and a proclamation about the social, relational and personal nature of our humanness'.[28] He is, of course, writing about the daily or weekly acts of worship or liturgy of a religious community. It may be strange to think that people who wouldn't entertain the thought of attending regular church activities will gladly and willingly take part in any meaningful ritual following an accident. There is at heart, I would suggest, a need to express our common humanity when threat or crisis looms large.

Those from a Protestant and evangelical position (and I write from such a stance) will point to the denunciation by the prophets of the false and empty rituals of Israel (Jeremiah 7, etc.). We will rightly criticise from a biblical standpoint anything that smacks of idolatry or dull repetition, where Christ is honoured just in word rather than in deed.

Along with others we will attempt to challenge the demands made on us by the outside world to de-Christianize our rituals, or to adopt the demands of the moment – to fit in with the outside world's view of Christian ministry. In the normal run of things these challenges may be faced over issues such as requiring preparation of parents before a child is baptised, or over the remarriage of divorcees, or over an appropriate inscription on a tombstone in a churchyard, etc.

An individual or corporate rite is demanded of the church because that is what it supposedly is in the business of offering. However, when the reasons for the request are challenged, then a quite different response may be evoked: people may decide to 'shop around' at other churches, and may make the accusation, 'You are driving people away from your church, vicar!' The notion that God's church was a kind of 'spiritual shop' was repugnant to Luther and the early reformers, but in a milder form we sometimes offer something similar. We may not recognise what we are doing and may well rightly laud the evangelistic and pastoral opportunities it gives. However, shops exist where there is a demand, and in the secular though not totally de-Christianized mind, the church can be seen as a kind of spiritual shop – a highly specialised one, of course. I may visit the supermarket once or twice a week but I may only consult a solicitor once or twice in a lifetime. Yet both are there to respond to human need. Other agencies may have in part surplanted the churches' traditional role of counsel and comfort in times of crisis, but in terms of organised ritual following a disaster the Church of God (and especially the Church of England) usually has a real role to play. The pressure to limit the church to that role alone has of course to be firmly resisted!

So a personal dilemma arises, a dilemma which I suggest occurs quite frequently when the church offers ministry not to its own members but to a secular society which, although claiming in many ways to believe in God, actually acts in a contrary way. This may take the form of a request (on sometimes strong demand) for a particular song which is in Christian terms quite unsuitable or in the matter of a funeral the minister may be manipulated so that the secular world presses in upon God's church at the heart of its ministry. In the church it is not a case of the 'customer is always right'. We do not say this in terms of the patient/doctor relationship and we should not say it in terms of the parishioner/minister relationship. 'Emotional blackmail' can be a very powerful weapon at times like these and God's ministers are not always the best judges of such pressures. That is not to say there should not be a discernment and response to 'felt needs'. Of course, this is right and proper but the Church of God does have a distinctive role to play. There is a fine line between responding to real requests for help and having your role manipulated, and this is especially true when it comes to ritual.

In our local situation, following the crash in Akers Way, Swindon, there were a variety of expressions of ritual. They involved people simply standing around the accident site and the piling of flowers on the spot. More bizarre was the nocturnal throwing of five damaged teddy bears into the garden of the common law wife of the accused driver. More significant was the demonstration march from the church along Akers Way at 8.00 a.m. on the following Wednesday when some 800 people turned up to walk in silence with linked arms across the road, to the spot where the children were killed. The initial intention of the organizers (the newly formed Moredon Safety Group) was to give expression to anger and grief, and to serve notice to the local authorities about the need for greater safety resources along that stretch of road and in Swindon as a whole. However, it soon became an expression of local mourning and, far from being an expression of violent anger, a certain dignity was apparent. My fellow team vicar and I were robed, and we linked arms with complete strangers. Warnings about unseemly behaviour and how it would be reported in the media were heeded. The police closed the road for its entire length and, when the procession reached the accident spot the names of the victims were read out, prayers were said, together with a reading of Psalm 23, and Christian expression of acute grief and emotion made clear.

There was also the opportunity to take school assemblies at the junior and infant schools on the Monday following the accident. Regrettably, a similar such offer to the local secondary school was politely rebuffed.

Preaching on such occasions is extremely demanding, but a glorious opportunity. The ability to listen and absorb God's word at such times is clearly very difficult and it is often remarked that the way the ritual is conducted speaks more loudly than the words uttered. Nevertheless God needs to speak his Word into such situations even if the messenger feels inadequate for them. It made very little difference that none of the bereaved families, at that time, had any commitment to Christian worship (see postscript). One family who, initially, wanted the service to be held at the cemetery chapel was easily persuaded to have a service in St Mary's, mainly on the grounds of needing to accommodate so many people.

Also loosely included under this heading of ritual was the siting of the graves in the local authority cemetery. A site was found where four of the victims could be buried together, and daily visits to the graves became, at least in the first instance, very much part of the lifestyle and private ritual of some of the victims' families, with quantities of flowers and various toys to left there.

St Mary's Church was made available each afternoon for prayer and comfort as needed, and great use was made of this facility by school-friends, teachers, friends, families and the community at large as a place where they felt able to express their grief and feelings without restraint or question. This facility has in time become part of the life of the church, albeit now on a much smaller scale.

Obviously the liturgy of the parish church was affected by the tragic events a few hundred yards away, the victims' families being encouraged to attend the following Sunday and over subsequent weeks. Unbeknown to each other, both families of victim and relatives of the driver attended the same act of worship. Not only the atmosphere of worship but the prayers and preaching were considerably influenced by what had happened so recently and so locally. It is difficult to judge how it affected attendance; perhaps a few who had heard what had happened felt the need to come on Sundays and, contrary to their normal lifestyle, to join in worship. Perhaps one or two came out of curiosity. There is obviously a need to adapt and respond to such an incident but there is also a need for normality. Other people's spiritual needs have to be catered for regardless of the major event of the time.

Looking back, the diary for that period records such events as a 'March for Jesus' day, a sponsored cycle ride, three weddings at the parish church, a Sunday School outing and, not least, the tenth anniversary celebrations of our sister church one and a half miles away. This shows that in some ways normal parish life went on as usual but the tragedy was very much in the hearts and minds of regular worshippers over that period. For those leading worship it is a matter of fine judgment in order to be sensitive to people's needs, sensitive to the Holy Spirit, and thus able to achieve the right balance of acknowledgement of an event which is dominating the life of the community around. Unless the church is especially eclectic it will be offering Christians drawn from that community a great deal. On the other hand the ordained ministry and the worship must address all the other things happening in people's lives which are quite 'normal'.

There is, of course, not only a need for balance but also for honest learning which allows for weeping, for anger, for expression of emotion and for healing. Ritual, whether it is a responsive 'first aid' to outsiders or whether it is the habit and practice of normal Sundays, must be real. I would rue the day when anyone is regarded as a spiritual 'customer' or 'consumer' but in a sense there are people like that, asking for needs to be met and also willing to give something to God in return. Obviously there can be little in terms of preparation for such ritual. (However, the Book of Common Prayer in the 'Forms of prayer to be used at sea' does have a short prayer which includes the words 'hear, hear us and save us that we perish not'. There is also the rubric 'When there shall be imminent danger . . . the ship shall be called together and make an humble Confession of their sin to God'. But such crisis liturgy is not the norm nor can it really be planned for in advance. However, as disaster upon disaster is portrayed in the media it ought, I suggest, to be a cause for enhanced awareness both pastorally and liturgically by minister and congregations alike. As far as I am aware, no 'spiritual' disaster plan exists but we can all ask ourselves the question: How should I as a minister, how should we as a Christian community, respond were a disaster to occur on our doorstep today? The vital, outward concern of every local church is then brought into question and exposed to the watching world. Much has been made over the past fifty years about William Temple's great adage that the 'church exists primarily for the sake of those who are not its members'. Yet in reality the opposite is often found to be true; but woe betide that Christian community when disaster strikes for such inward-looking congregations have little to offer the needy pain-ridden world. Then people turn elsewhere for spiritual comfort and help, and another nail is hammered in the coffin of the institutional church.

However, there are countless examples of situations where God's people are not closed and inward-looking, where there is alertness to what God may be doing outside the formal structures and to the kaleidoscope of both physical, mental and spiritual human needs. Such a response is of course 'kingdom enhancing' rather than 'kingdom retarding' and is tangible proof of a God who does intervene in the day-to-day lives of people and situations. Many situations seem at first sight beyond human control but in reality they can be brought within the sovereignty of Christ as Lord.

A year after the accident plans for an ecumenical act of worship were discussed by local clergy, since the exact day and time coincided with many Sunday evening services. However, these plans were soon dropped when it became known that some of the victims' families did not want to participate. Instead they, along with representatives of the emergency services and the Mayor of Thamesdown, were invited to attend the usual evening service at St Mary's. This service seemed in some ways to mark not only the anniversary of a year since the accident had occurred but also an endorsement that phase one of the grieving process was now over.

Prior to the service, the Moredon Safety Group, which had sprung up as a result of the accident but had now sadly shrunk to a few members, arranged for a memorial stone to be placed on the exact spot of the accident. My colleague and I were invited to dedicate it three days before the anniversary of the deaths. The stone, which is perhaps not to everyone's taste, is in black marble and arguably somewhat over-large for its purpose – a local teenager thought some of the victims had been reburied on the site! So ritual of some sort gave expression to both personal and public grief. Two of the events organised by those outside the church membership in the local community also involved Christian liturgical rites.

However, we do need to revisit the question of whether ritual is based on some form of psychological need or whether it is of prime theological importance.

The secularist might well argue that a ritual is merely a means of trying to express the inexpressible, of acting out something when words seem redundant, or at least devising a form of words and actions which express a reality and which in the majority of cases portray what might have happened or is in the process of taking place. In situations where men and women are confronted by mystery, or the need to establish order, or to make some sort of corporate expression, is it merely a psychological device to provide meaningful order? Elaine Ramshaw has stated, 'without ritualisation we would have to plan every action from scratch and analyse the meaning of every interaction like the stereo-typed psychoanalyst who responds to "Hello" by saying "What do you mean by that?"'[29]

Certainly it would seem true in part that some rituals in charismatic worship are a right reaction to the over-complicated and continuous analysis which some Christian leaderships have indulged in. Simply to enjoy the experience of God's power, either putting aside complicated questions or pretending they do not exist, is one of many responses that can be made in situations which have become over-formalised or over-familiar or have lost their power.

However, a key question arises at this point: is the (Christian) minister just there to provide some focus for the ritualisation of events or does he or she have a wider role? Put another way, is the Christian minister there just to meet certain needs in the community, as a witch doctor might do in other societies?

From a gospel standpoint it would seem that the role of the Christian minister is as a leader of a community of faith, with clear demarcation lines between believers who belong and unbelievers who don't. However historic Anglicanism does not recognise such a clear division. This may have been viable in days when our society or country could be called 'Christian', but now the status quo has changed. But, are we to deny requests from outside the Christian community? Or, are we to be selective i.e. by setting out our criteria for marrying divorcees, or by baptising infants.

Some time ago, Iona and Peter Opie wrote, 'English people will often readily believe in the supernatural provided it is not part of the Bible or the institutionalised spirituality of the church'.[30] This is still largely true. There is evidence that a few people sought help from some form of spiritualism after the Akers Way tragedy. However, it was the closeness and easy availability of support from the established church which was readily accepted.

By 'coincidence', the local Evangelical Alliance prayer breakfast occurred both on the Saturday morning on the day after the accident and again on the Saturday morning on the day before the anniversary, which could also come under the heading of ritual. However, on a personal level, it was more of pastoral support to my wife and myself. Indeed, also other prayer meetings and staff meetings, which were part of the life of the churches, perhaps came under the heading of support rather than ritual.

Specifically Christian ritual gives clarity and some degree of purpose to events which seem totally devastating and meaningless. It gives opportunity to a clear and sympathetic presentation of the Good News of Jesus for ultimately, of course, little can be understood of tragic death apart from the cross of Jesus Christ.

There is one area of ritual which is hard to record, and this is the matter of private prayer. For many without much experience of Christian life it will be simply a time of silence. I can do no better than to repeat the words of Alan Billings after the Hillsborough tragedy: 'These ritual acts were the prayers of the inarticulate and the prayers of those for whom any words that might be said would not be good enough. Those of us who set great store by words and live so much of our lives in heads full of them can sometimes be very dismissive of the ritual of folk or common religion. After Hillsborough that which is usually well hidden stood revealed: people need appropriate ritual to put them in touch with their deepest emotions and so with God.'

With two of the three schools adjacent to the site involving clergy in school assemblies, and the junior school choir singing at the double funeral etc., there were many expressions of community grief. Grief couched in at least seven public ritual events, two within schools and countless others of a private or semi-private nature. They at least gave some sense of meaning and purpose in the face of tragedy. Could they have been carried out better? The answer is, of course, they could have been, but in spite of a wealth of experience it was not something that could be reasonably anticipated nor its communal response be planned in advance.

10

What is the Effect on Community Life?

This was the recurring question put by representatives of the media, and it was a legitimate question. In the first place they wanted to know about the community itself, not for any sociological reasons, but as good background material to their accounts. In my position as Team Rector of the parish I seemed to be seen as some kind of spokesperson. It is I think, worth noting that the old railway town of Swindon is part of Thamesdown which has a total population of around 160,000 people. It is a town which has seen a number of waves of expansion, principally from London overspill in the 1950s and from a great deal of private development in the 1980s. In the area of Akers Way, however, although a number of residents have purchased their properties, almost all of the dwellings are owned by the local authority. It is an area which would not be offended to be called 'middle working class'. However, it does not have the cohesion of, say, a traditional village or some other council estates in Swindon or elsewhere. Nevertheless, it does have some sense of community of which three schools and the local parish church are the only visible symbols. Moredon community centre, although built to serve the needs of the area, is some way from the site of the accident.

Certainly when crises occur a community comes together in a sense of shared anger, shock and grief. An immediate tangible evidence of this was in the collecting of monies for the bereaved families. Three such efforts were made, the chief one being sponsored by the Mayor of Thamesdown. The sense of helplessness that many people feel on such occasions is alleviated a little, perhaps, by contributing to an urgent emotive appeal. No enquiry seems to have been made about whether there was actual financial need; certainly, in Swindon, a large number of people contributed, even if some could only make a very small donation.

A local musician produced a record, the sale of which eventually produced some money for the relatives. The Safety Group came into being and their fund-raising efforts were largely spent on the memorial stone. As with any observed bereavement, there is often the feeling of 'What can I do to help?', to which the logical answer is often 'nothing or very little' especially if the people concerned are, themselves, in a state of shock or on the periphery of events. Obviously too, in an event such as this, some form of political action often takes place; in our situation it was expressed it the protest march, which turned into a memorial service. However, the petitioning of the local council, and attendance at its meetings when feelings were running very high, were all expressions of the anger and frustration by those able to articulate the feelings of many.

Within a few months, the speed limit was lowered to 30 m.p.h., double white lines were painted on the road, and a sign was placed at each end of Akers Way saying 'Kill your speed not a child'. The latter was soon removed after protests by some of the families involved. Twelve months later a roundabout was constructed, which will also have the effect of slowing the traffic considerably.

But the community to which I am referring has a more formal expression, such as in the make-up of schools or factories, the members of the local church and church families as well as other ad hoc groupings.

Whilst, indeed, many people were deeply affected by the tragedy others, either depending on their closeness to the event, or to relatives, saw it as much more marginal to their lives. To judge from the reactions of members of St Mary's church with a membership of 250 adults, there was also a sense of confusion and loss. This arose partly from Christian concern, heightened by the fact that teachers of the children from the schools involved were part of our church family. Our church membership is largely local, and is drawn from a sizeable parish of 23,000 but with very few active members coming from the area of the accident itself.

The fact that church members took time off work to provide

stewarding in the church for the funerals showed considerable commitment to intense local need. It also became very apparent that St Mary's church fulfils its role as the parish church and not just as a gathering place of the faithful. This came as something of a surprise to some members of the church community who see the church building used for an average of fifty funerals per year and about the same number of weddings per year. The church is also able to serve the community through schools' educational visits, carol services etc., and this has meant a fairly high profile in the community, in contrast to some other urban churches. St Mary's church membership felt, for a time, the pain and loss of some of those who were not yet its active members and this was, in a sense deeply sacramental. Despite the anger in the wider community, the need to be brothers and sisters in Christ was very apparent in much of the life of the Church. The church is a community where, above all else, the very best in neighbourliness needs to be expressed. In saying this I do not wish to decry kindness or expressions of similar neighbourliness that were shown elsewhere, but the Christian faith is nothing if it does not show itself in a loving caring community.

Sadly, apart from the immediate sharing by the sister church one and a half miles away which is part of our team, the local Evangelical Alliance and other neighbourhood churches, little support was offered by the deanery or diocese. The rural dean and one other local incumbent did ring with words of hope and encouragement. The then diocesan communications officer, by virtue of the office, was also in contact within twenty-four hours of the accident. The tragedy, of course, was not big enough to fall into the category of a 'major' disaster but for many of us involved that was not the issue, other brief phone calls, notes asssuring prayers would have made all the difference at the time, and also twelve months later at the Crown Court trial. The backup systems in other professions show up the weakness of the church's organisation. Of all the full-time 'ministries' to use that overworked word in its widest sense, the ordained clergy should have the best available *organised* care for the carers. However, within the Church of England, there are signs of improvement in this area but it would still seem to vary from diocese to diocese.

Certainly, in theory, there exists a system of care from parish, through deanery and archdeaconry to the bishop himself. However, the cry 'who cares for the carers?' is still often heard amongst clergy who, if serving on their own, can feel lonely and vulnerable in their everyday work for God.

The system of week in, week out care will obviously vary from diocese to diocese, but often it seems assumptions are made which side-step the really important questions. The traditional model of Anglican clergy in an almost independent role has, of course, mitigated against any idea of 'control'. At the same time it has very often meant assumptions about work loads and stress which cannot be justified. The fact that many clergy now work in teams or groups should improve care and support for one another but, this can be a false assumption, not least because of the nature and style of many team and group ministries. It also seems true that where clergy still work on their own, or in multiple 'patches', either because they choose to do so or find it difficult to work in a team, this can lead to extreme loneliness and the vulnerability that goes with such isolation. A better way forward might be to give greater authority and power to the rural dean. But how? Rural deans are usually chosen by the bishop after consultation with local clergy. Perhaps they should be chosen on their proven track record of care for their fellow clergy. If the archdeacon and bishop cannot (and in a few cases will not) give adequate care and support, then it seems logical for the person in that most ambivalent of roles, i.e. the rural dean, to be given greater responsibility in this area. With the advent of women priests in the Church of England the situation may well change. There could, of course, be situations where a single woman is left on her own in a parish or a group of parishes, and if she is a vulnerable person, she could risk being ever further isolated than perhaps a male priest in such a role.

To some degree, separation from the 'world' and sometimes the rest of the congregation, has led clergy into this trap. The very word 'priest' can invite ideas of separation and status which others in the church know little about. Clergy manners, dress, etc., can all lead to this 'caste' idea. Leadership itself can be a lonely situation. Nevertheless, where clergy are appreciated, loved and valued, and know it to be true, then the risk of breakdown is considerably lessened. A system of personal review of ministry, of individual spiritual directors and so on is fine and often works well, but for some it smacks of interference, so often ministers are their own worst enemies!

Some of what I have said is rather speculative. The only evidence I have to support lapses in care by others is to point to how few pastoral visits I have had from bishops over my time in the ordained ministry. Two or three, to be precise! Morale in a business or industry could hardly survive for long if the manager is seen on the shop floor so infrequently. In a 'care industry' such as the church where the products are love, peace and concern for others, it does seem quite indefensible. Certainly, with hindsight, in the weeks around September 1991 there was little evidence of such care by the bishop(s) and the then archdeacon. This, as it is written some years later, may seem somewhat critical, but a phone call here, a half hour visit there, would have made all the difference!

Perhaps more needs to be thought and done about the patchiness of pastoral care of those in the ordained ministry. With ever-tightening financial stringencies on the horizon more than a few articulate voices will rightly demand value for money from those in full time service. Justification of how time is spent will be expected by congregations paying higher and higher 'quotas'. However, if that demand is not tempered with real Christian love, then conflicts could easily arise. At one point, when working in the East Hull clergy team, all four of us kept diaries of work-time. They were very revealing! Not in terms of laziness or industry but how actually we spent our time in the task we were called to do.

On a personal note, I do value the enormous independence the ordained ministry gives; an independence which has, in the past been stoutly defended. What other job has such freedom? We operate under a system of divine grace which is right and good. We have no day to day answerability as is the experience of most people in the secular world nor are we motivated by profit, so the level of individual responsibility and care is all the more important when such freedom in employment exists.

In a ministry situation, the best system I have experienced is the one of 'deanery days' where the bishop and the archdeacon spend a whole day in the deanery. Visits to local industry and schools, etc., are punctuated by time with clergy wives, individual interviews, and the day perhaps ends with a Confirmation service and this all helps in the process of caring. A system such as this can surely help to improve crisis management.

The fact that the Akers Way tragedy remained on the agenda of school governors' meetings, church councils, residents' associations etc., for a considerable time, showed how much it affected the community as a whole. Also the local Swindon papers, including the *Evening Advertiser* and the local radio stations BBC Wiltshire Sound and GWR commercial radio, kept the issue and the subsequent trial very much alive in the minds and hearts of both the local and the wider community.

Later in the chapter there is a record of some of the interviews with children who were witnesses to the tragedy but, not so immediately obvious, was the effect on the education of some of the 1400 children who attend the three schools adjacent to the accident site. There was a measurable decline in exam results at the seconday school, even though the tests were taken quite some time after the accident itself. It was obvious to the staff of the junior and infant schools that because of the resulting absenteeism and disruptive behaviour of quite a few children, their educational progress was hindered. What measures could be taken to offset this, I would not wish to hazard. From my own experience spending formative years at school when some lessons were taken in an air raid shelter, and the war dominated most of life, I have come to realise now how much it affected my own learning process. For all that, I cannot give it as an excuse for failing the 11+ twice. However I felt for a long while I was always trying to catch up on other people's learning. Maybe, in the future, some of the children in the Moredon area of Swindon will have to spend such 'catching up time' as I and thousands of other war children have done. It is not just about a desire to learn, but having to cope with the feeling that quite a few others are ahead of you in the educational stakes. This seems to be a further aspect of a violent interruption in the path of educational progress.

Unfortunately such is human nature that it is often the case that many of the intense feelings of goodwill and neighbourliness eventually evaporate. It is the continuing pastoral and evangelistic task of the church, when no great crisis exists, to encourage such attitudes and to ensure that the local Christian church is the best model available of community life. In some cases a sense of 'belonging' comes before 'believing', however important we see Christian doctrine to be.

Two other aspects of 'community' need to be recorded. Because four of the victims' families were living in local authority properties adjacent or near the site of the accident, they were soon offered the possibility of rehousing which they were able to take up. The family of the two injured, who lived 200 yards from the site, were already in the process of moving house and, although delayed by the accident, eventually moved to another part of Swindon. The other family have every intention of staying where they are, a few yards away from the scene of the disaster.

Of the two drivers charged and convicted of driving offences, the parents of the main culprit still live within a few hundred yards of the site, whilst the other driver is still living about half a mile from the spot.

It is laudable that the local authority recognised the emotions of the victims' families and responded to the fact that the site itself can produce considerable fears within them, and hence the desire to move away. In a previous parish, a regular member of our tiny congregation would never walk past a spot, just around the corner from her home, since it was the site where her husband had been killed some years before. Perhaps there needs to be a ministry of exorcising such sites before people have to uproot from their homes and neighbourhoods.

C.S. Lewis wrote: 'An odd by-product of my loss is that I'm aware of being an embarrassment to everyone I meet. At work, at the club, in the street, I see people, as they approach me, trying to make up their minds whether they'll "say something about it" or not. I hate it if they do, and if they don't. Some funk it altogether . . . Perhaps the bereaved ought to be isolated in special settlements like lepers.'[31]

How true this was for the victims' families is hard to assess. Perhaps in this extreme situation it did not happen to quite the same degree, nevertheless the eventual commitment and involvement in the local church of at least three of the victims' parents showed that there was a need not met in the local community, to which the life of the local church and its ministry in the gospel was able to offer a response.

Mention has already been made that community bonding is

often a positive but transient fact of grief. In the long run, it is the more permanent aspects of that bonding that really count.

For the period of the trial at Gloucester Crown Court the police offered transport each day for the victims' families, an offer which was gladly accepted. Sitting in a police van for an hour each way for eleven days cemented relationships in a very real way. There was even considerable laughter at times amid the obvious tension. It was a trial that attracted a great deal of local interest and the resulting verdict was the first item on both the BBC and ITV early evening news broadcasts.

So, through the shared pain, considerable anger, grief, and bewilderment a sense of community spirit at various depths was created and this spirit was expressed in both formal and informal ritual. At times, this spirit was expressed in disagreement over what action should be taken regarding road safety and what should be the appropriate punishment for the drivers involved. Although in some cases this spirit evaporated fairly quickly, nevertheless some lasting friendships were made, some goals achieved in terms of improved driving standards and safety measures. It is always the mark of a Christian perspective that these positive aspects are dwelt upon. The Church, the sign and symbol of the new community, had its part to play both through its membership and through the committed, caring involvement of its ordained ministry.

On 4 October, 1993, at the Appeal Court in London, Shaun Gooch appeared to appeal against his sentence of five years and three months imposed at Gloucester Crown Court twelve months previously. The Lord Chief Justice, Lord Taylor, sitting with two other Appeal Judges, upheld the conviction, but agreed that the three-month sentence which had been imposed, because Gooch was banned from driving when the accident occurred, could now run concurrently. Lord Taylor concluded that 'This was a multiple death case in which these young people were cut off from the rest of their lives by this appalling driving. We do not consider five years was inappropriate in this case'.

Considerable media coverage resulted in local interviews expressing buried anger amongst some residents living near the crash site. However, none of the bereaved families were interviewed or expressed opinions publicly. At the same time (two years after the accident) compensation claims were still being pursued by solicitors acting on behalf of three of the families, due to negotiations between two insurance companies.

In an accident such as has been described, it is the effect on children that is the most marked and will probably have the most lasting effect.

At the time of the accident, the acting head of Moredon Infants' School said her feeling was that many of the youngest children did not, in fact, witness the event but those who did seemed to have a 'matter of fact' approach to it because they simply did not understand what happened. This was despite the fact that the youngest victim had only recently moved from the Infant School to the Juniors. The initial assembly following 13 September, 1991, was the most difficult. Some of the children seemed to be very quiet for some while afterwards, but it was amongst the staff that the effect was felt most acutely.

The impact in the adjoining Junior School was markedly different. Here, more children had actually witnessed the event, and two of the pupils had been killed. The head teacher, described the initial assembly (where indeed I was present and spoke to the staff and pupils) as 'the worst assembly of my life'. There had been wide consultation over the weekend following the crash. The local primary school adviser manned the telephone on the Monday morning though, initially, there was very little media attention. The plan was to try and function as normal. The staff were highly supportive of each other. However, the governing body was *not* called upon to meet. The head teacher stopped writing her log book and only recommenced it a year later.

The pupils reacted initially with considerable flatness and there was a 'strange eerieness' about the building. Approximately thirty children were withdrawn by the staff from classes. At that stage no anger was expressed though subsequent acts of vandalism both in and out of school hours may well have been expressions of latent feelings. There were, indeed, changes in playground behaviour with 'strange' games being evolved which eventually turned to become more aggressive. This latent anger was still being expressed in disruptive behaviour some eighteen months after the accident by children who witnessed the event and, sadly, their parents were not as co-operative as they might have been.

She does point to positive gain in improvements in staff relationships and pupil/staff relationships. There is, however, a feeling of 'wanting to put it all behind them' whilst, at the same time, there are constant reminders of the event e.g. the memorial stone, shaped so much like a grave that more than one child has enquired if the victims have been reburied there! Certain hymns used in assembly, deaths of pets or bereavements in the family, the church building, visits by the clergy can all be 'trigger' memories.

The following report has been produced by John Spanton nurse therapist, (Child and Family Guidance) and I am reproducing it with his permission. It underlines the overriding twin lessons which can be learnt from such an event: the long-term support of the bereaved and injured; and adequate debriefing for those involved in caring.

Akers Way Accident

Six children pulled chairs up into a tight circle. As it was a school staff-room, a previously prohibited place, they had chosen the chairs to make a point, rather than sitting on the floor. There was a bit of shuffling and giggling as introductions were made and they moved on to the business of why they had been brought together.

Major tragedy had devastated a community which was situated on the edge of a medium-sized town based in a large 1950s council housing estate. Five of their children were dead, and it happened on a main road where nearly everyone walked or drove to school. Nobody in the community was untouched by this tragedy and, because the accident was the result of illegal road-racing, the anger was great and people seemed to have difficulty in finding a focus for this anger.

Petitions, placards and protest marches didn't seem to do the job and the anger then turned inwards and for six months the schools received, almost nightly, vandalism and theft. Of the three schools, infant, junior and secondary, the junior school was bearing the brunt of these attacks, and that was also the school which had asked for help for their children.

Thirty children had been identified as having particular problems and so, four days after the accident, these children were split into groups of five and six so that they could all have some time with a counsellor.

An attempt was made to link the children in the groups with others who had had similar experiences of the accident. For instance one group was for children who had witnessed the full horrors at or soon after the occurrence, and another was for children who had close contact with any of the victims, like sitting next to them in school, or being friends of the family. The idea being that the detail of work necessary for one group would not be relevant to another and so the approach would be different.

However, as time went by it emerged that some children had feigned involvement (but not distress), for complex reasons, mainly concerning loss and deprivation in their lives. They left the groups when this was discovered. Other children were stopped attending by their parents. The groups stopped working as the counsellors felt the children were coping, the longest one running for ten sessions.

The groups all started with an attempt to debrief the children. They were given the opportunity to talk about where they were at the time of the accident – if they were on the site, what they saw, the smells, the sounds, and their feelings. Other groups concentrated on where the children were when they heard the accident, what their feelings were at that time.

The groups all developed in different ways, some children finding the idea quite difficult and wanting to disrupt the process; other groups became much more vital to the children who were in them and one of these is described in more detail.

This group contained the children who had been at the site of the accident or arrived at it soon after. There they had witnessed a number of occurrences which were almost outside their understanding: the instant death of a friend two yards from where she had been standing; smashed and mangled bodies; an arm severed; adults arriving on the scene and becoming out of control; emergency services arriving and taking a long time to deal with them; the injured; the screams; and a trapped child.

Some children ran away from the scene while others stood transfixed until parents or other adults took them away. It was never clear how long each child had remained at the scene – they were all completely uninjured and some had remained a distance away and some, as mentioned, were not there at all but pretended to have been involved and used what they had heard in the playground and from their parents talking to describe the scene.

The reasons for these children wanting to do this were complex, but in this group of six children four of them had previously experienced a violent or sudden death in their close family and this soon came out in the sessions that followed. This proved quite a difficulty as the group was set up to allow the children to make some sense of the scene they had witnessed. However, it is not possible to deny past life experiences, so these deaths were used in the process of the group and the individual needs of the children in this respect were not pursued.

Individual sessions for these children would have been ideal but when large numbers have to be seen the group situation is the only way of dealing with it. The difficulties are that unless really carefully selected, children will hear details from each other which they don't necessarily need to hear if they hadn't all experienced the same traumas and also could use the group for reasons for which it wasn't set up.

The weekly pattern for these eight and nine year olds developed with a theme for each week – painting and colouring were an integral part of the process but the difficulties with this were that once one child had chosen to develop a theme in a particular way the spontaneity for the others was lost and they would copy the idea and therefore the drawings could all look quite the same.

The children did appear to benefit from the group process but for various reasons it was not possible to follow up the groups and the work finished leaving many questions unanswered and some children still in need of further therapy.

Lessons and ideas from this experience would lead to a different plan if similar circumstances arose in the future.

When a large number of children are affected by a disaster or tragedy, groups will be necessary, as individual counselling, particularly in the early stages, will not be practicable.

If confronted with a similar occurrence, where the work

would be based on a school, the following guidelines should be followed.

1. Co-operation from the school is essential. At a time of major trauma and high drama, the normal school leadership processes might not be working well and therefore it is important that there is a system which takes over and all the decisions can be made which would be most helpful for the long-term health of all those involved in the school – this would include having parents' meetings, access to the children, planning classroom work around the children's traumas, and longer-term anniversary work and discussions.

2. Debriefing groups for children should be set up within three days of the trauma and be available for all those who were closely involved with the event.

3. Discussions with staff and with those running the debriefing sessions should meet and select children for groups for ongoing work.

4. These groups should start as soon as possible and be run by people skilled in group dynamics and use all the techniques and systems appropriate for the age-group.

5. Support for the teachers should be available, particularly to allow them to examine some of the issues that have arisen from the disaster in the classroom in an appropriate way.

6. Children with very particular difficulties should be referred on for individual therapy.

7. Parent groups might be an important part of this process so that they will have some understanding of the work that the children are doing.

Children's Letters to Jesus

Another facet of the effect on children was the spiritual understanding by the children of this dreadful event. With the co-operation of the Junior School head-teacher children were invited to 'write a letter to Jesus' which they could post in a box in school. This method has, of course, long been used in children's missions but that was not the aim here. It was used to enable those most deeply affected to express their view of 'Where God was last Friday'. These letters were written and collected over a period of four weeks after the event.

TO sheree I
hope you are
o Kay

love
Jemma
Scatt
xx

To Jesus

    I am write to Shere and Ian I ~~mast~~ miss them alot they we friend ~~oof~~ of my and my sisster. Tell Shere that I love her and that I miss her alot this is a Sad time for her family and her school mates and he School Teacher.

    P.S.   Shirley

To Jesus

Wish The peoples
parants a wish
for me.

pleaSe make

sure That my

BesT friend Sherry
and my friend
Ian my friend
Belinda and
everyone one
who was in The

Taragic accident
Love from Joanna
xxx

Dear Sheree
           I am writting to tell you I am sorry you had to leave us so soon. We were good friends and I will miss you very much. I have got your picture in my bible by my bed, so I know you are safe now, In Jesus's home in heaven, I am saying prayers for you at night so I hope you can hear me.
           Goodbye Sheree untill we all meet again one day.
                 God Bless you.
           Love from your friend + next door neighbour
                      Matthew Strange.
           X X X   X X X.

Dear Jesus and sherry and god
I would Like to say things about My feeling's
aBout the Accident. I'm very upset about
the children who died in the Accedent
and the pupul in hospital. I Loued every
one in a way and why did you take
them up So urly in heven I kno you Should
have taken them instead of Beaing in
Agoney in hospital that was the Best thing
to do. all I would Like to say is it was
very Sad and hurtruk for every one
esPeshaly for the Perents and Relashions
Just tell them I miss you alot and love
you espeshally cherry leas We all miss you.

Loue to heven Jesus and God and to
you. thankyou for Beaing understanding
god and Jesus.

Gemma Lewis Loving you all
    Sorry about the sPeiling mastakes

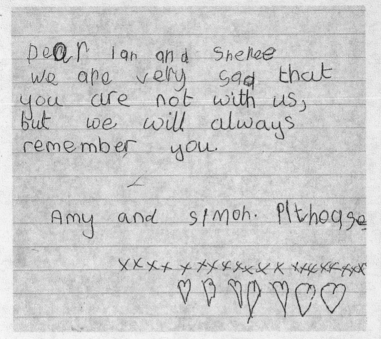

Dear Ian and Shelee
we are very sad that
you are not with us,
but we will always
remember you.

Amy and simon. Pithogge

xxxx x xxxxxx x x xxxxxxxxx
♡ ♡ ♡♡ ♡♡♡

What the letters reveal about children's spiritual understanding of a tragic event is for others to surmise but a significant number of them were written by some of the least able children. Literate expression of grief was obviously not confined to those best able to express it on paper.

11

Has God forgotten us?

If we were able to track God down, if He was in an inescapable position where He had to answer our question, 'Where have you been?', what would His reply be? The simple answer is that He has been here all the time, only we have failed to recognise Him! The beauty of His creation is often so disfigured by man that we are not able to see His handiwork. Human beings are crushed through sin and violence, and God's image is lost from sight. The Church, the one body commissioned to reflect His Son, spends so much time on itself and its own internal disputes, that others cannot see Jesus. The moral (or immoral) stance of many does nothing to promote the love of God in Christ, and so on. It is a dreary catalogue of both individual and corporate sin. As a confession in the Alternative Service Book says, 'We have marred your image in us'.

Yet all is not without hope. The love of God is discernible in a million kind deeds, a thousand and one hugs and not least in the worship of those who are committed to Christ. Every day there are an estimated 7,000 new Christian converts; in the main as the result of the proclamation of the gospel and the effect of lively Spirit-filled worship.

However, as I reflect on the accident of that September evening in 1991 I have to face up to a number of possibilities. The first is to see it solely in terms of judgement. None of the people involved were, in my view, committed Christians. Could this have been the judgement of God upon people who ignore and disobey Him? After all, God meted out judgement on Sodom and Gomorrah in the Old Testament. The book of Revelation is full of pictures such as these. Harsh and cruel as it may seem, some people in the Church come to this conclusion.

Any calamity and disaster is viewed as a logical consequence of human sin. God is judge and, despite the youthful innocence of the victims, He will act in this way. Moreover, it is seen as a warning to others to repent before it is too late, to turn from their wickedness before the same or a similar fate befalls them as well.

Such a case can clearly be made from some biblical teaching, but is that the whole picture? If it is true, then the only picture of God that emerges is of a cold, cruel, heartless, judgemental Being bent on extracting vengeance. However, such a view does ignore the truth that Christians are not immune to catastrophe and accident. There is no automatic insurance that when people become Christians they are either exempt from prolonged suffering or will automatically escape the accidents which befall the human race. As far as I am aware there are no statistics to show that Christian people have a greater life expectancy than others. They may, and should, drive more carefully. They may, and should, be just as safety conscious as others. They may see the human body in a different way to many unbelieving people. They will not regard it uniquely as a receptacle for the 'soul' but will consider it to be special because of Jesus' incarnation. Well-being of the Spirit does not mean neglect of the body. Indeed it may, and should, mean an enhanced view of the body as described in the New Testament. 'Do you not know that your body is a temple of the Holy Spirit.' (1 Cor. 6:19) Paul's use of the word 'temple' sees the body as holy, not just as a container for the Spirit. When such a view prevails it means activities such as sex, exercise, eating habits, sleep, relaxation, can all be seen in a holistic way which gives them (or lack of them) a truly Christian perspective. However, despite such teaching, in many cases the Church has not taken on board the biblical view of the body, and consequently other organisations and philosophies have attempted to fill the gap. Nature is said to abhor a vacuum, and this seems equally true in the spiritual realm. Nevertheless, when all this is taken into account it does not necessarily mean any special protection for the Christian!

In the course of writing this book and in the months after the accident in September 1991, two events occurred in Rodbourne Cheney which highlight this issue. In January 1993 as remedial work was being carried out on the south side of the chancel to St Mary's Church, the area was wreathed in scaffolding and corrugated steel sheeting. During the course of a parade service with numerous childen's organisations present, and the creche full of tiny infants, a high wind ripped much of this cladding apart tearing two stone pinnacles from the roof and sending them crashing down to land just above the heads of the clergy leading the worship. A lucky escape, or the hand of a loving God intervening to protect His people?

Certainly, if it had happened ten minutes later when the congregation were leaving the building, a major disaster could have taken place. As it was, the fire brigade spent most of the Sunday afternoon making the building safe and then prohibited its use for our Sunday evening worship. The latter did take place in our church hall, and took on a spirituality and vibrancy which, to say the least, was special to the occasion! Nevertheless, it was no coincidence that it occurred during the singing of 'Stand up, stand up for Jesus', particularly as the crash of stone, sheeting and scaffolding happened as we reached the words, 'This day the noise of battle, the next the victor's song'.

Eighteen months later, during the course of a wedding rehearsal the church was struck by lightning. I was standing near the chancel with the prospective bride and groom, brides-maids, page boy, parents, best man and families, explaining the procedures, when the flag-pole took the force of a million or so volts. For a micro-second, the building itself was shaken. Even more shaken was the wedding party. Praise God for lightning conductors! Comments made four years earlier that 'we have never been struck before, rector, so why do we need one now?' had failed to prevail when the church council was discussing its advisability, and the point was rather proved. What was God saying at that moment? To the couple concerned (who were not regular worshippers), to the congregation who did not learn about it until thirty-six hours later, and to myself as the minister?

There is, of course, no such thing as an 'incident free' church but, during my time in Swindon, we have had cause to wonder what will happen next? It is a lesson to take on board that God may not necessarily be responsible for events such as those described above or for major disasters but, as I have attempted to point out in Chapter 7, 'Finding God in a Crisis', there is much to learn from such events, either through the Holy Spirit speaking directly to those involved or, more probably, through the encouragement they bring for mature reflection which sees God's hand in it all.

I was often asked at the time, and am still occasionally reminded, how the accident affected me on a personal level. I have to reply it did, and still does, affect me a great deal. Of course I was not there at the time it happened, nor did I lose loved ones, nor do I live adjacent to the site and, more particularly, one day I shall cease to be rector of this parish. So there are a number of factors which distance me both emotionally and geographically from the event itself and its aftermath. Nevertheless, any pastor worth his salt does experience other people's pain. It is true my visits to the families have all but ceased. 'Normality' has returned and, although it may be a 'cliché', life has to go on.

Looking back over the years, I am glad to have written this book at this time and not to have rushed into print. It has given me time to reflect on a number of issues: the wonder of God's love; His calling of me of all people to serve Him; the various ways people cope with tragedy; how some make a Christian commitment which seems real and genuine at the time and then evaporates as so-called normality returns. I have been able to reflect, I hope objectively, on the kindness of many people as well as on the fact that an accident of this magnitude sifts people in remarkable ways.

In the course of writing this book the most difficult thing has been to articulate my own feelings. There is no doubt in my mind that the ministry I offered was welcomed and effective. This was born out by a letter received two years later, the genesis of which had been a considerable amount of publicity in the local media over a particular conflict in the church. I shall always be grateful to the anonymous people who wrote: '*Dear Rev and Mrs Crees, How soon people forget. You were there in the pain of Akers Way, you poured out gentleness, understanding, love and compassion, you poured oil on the grief and pain, you agonised with that community. Where are they now in your time of need! We prayed for you last night for the situation you find yourself in. God bless you both.*'

I cannot read that over without emotion and the occasional tear. Status, honour and the acclaim of others should never be part of the Christian life or ministry. Sadly, centuries of Christian history have shown some of the church and its leaders to be affected in that way. We have simply ignored the words of Jesus, 'Woe to you when all men speak well of you' (Luke 6:26).

However, I would not be human if at some time I had not felt the need to be appreciated, accepted and loved. The ordained ministry can, in some ways, be a hard task, and it is probably more difficult to proclaim God's word effectively now than it was only two decades ago. I hesitate to guess what it will be like for those who follow in my particular vocation. Nevertheless, the occasional encouraging hand, the loving look, as well as seeing people find a living faith in Christ, make it all more than worthwhile.

The last word must come from those most affected, those whose lives can never be the same: one mother described her tragedy as 'three long years of absolute hell'. I am only too well aware that the publication of this book may awaken memories and hurts which are being healed. However, I trust that for them and many others, it will be something which will help them to see afresh the love of God for each one of us and to find in Him that life and death do have purpose and meaning in an increasingly meaningless world.

Postscript

Where was God last Friday? On the first Good Friday there is no record of the disciples asking such a question. The disciples on the road to Emmaus (Luke 24:19–21) come some way along that line of enquiry. If, at the deepest level, the question seems unanswerable or if only provisional answers can be postulated, then another certain motif needs to be applied: as we have seen, it is 'resurrection'!

In the weeks and months that followed the Akers Way accident the role of caring people proved crucial. Some of their support was immensely helpful, some less so. It helped to dissipate anger, it provided shoulders on which to weep and places for quiet, and it gave a chance for wounds to heal. The wounds were reopened to some degree by the trauma of the Crown Court trial a year later. Nevertheless, without any pressure, four clear expressions of new Christian faith were made. Two of the most public of these were in a confirmation service nine months after the accident, though sadly they have not, as yet, matured into total Christian commitment. Why others have not responded in such a way remains a mystery. Certainly the Church which seems, on the whole, irrelevant to many people, has become a home and a family to suffering people. St Mary's, whose origins go back to the thirteenth century and perhaps long before, may possibly have not been involved in caring on such a scale before. The building stands as a symbol of God's timeless love. The monument on the site of the accident is a visible reminder to all who pass by of what happened on that terrible September evening. The emergency services have, naturally, gone on to other duties, the local authorities have endeavoured to ensure such an accident does not occur again, those prosecuted have been convicted, but the church building some 600 yards from the site remains. The biblical perspective is of course, that the church of Jesus is not the building in which regrettably too many British people seem to invest much emotional capital, but a spiritual community – a body and a family. Nevertheless, sited as it is, and through an extraordinary number of circumstances, the building has become a home and haven to all who desire to find meaning and purpose in life, especially in the face of suffering which is often so hard to explain or rationalise. Therein lies a real spiritual paradox. Without this particular building the Christian community would not exist in the way it does; but without the Christian community, the building is really only of aesthetic and historical significance.

The hope of the Christian gospel is that there is a 'good' remembrance that is neither denial of the pain nor morbid instrospection and life-consuming guilt. A paraphrase of Ecclesiastes 3 says that there is a time to remember and a time to forget. Freedom in Christ does not mean obliterating painful events or people from the mind and emotions; it does, however, mean holding such things in a right perspective and above all seeing God's love and care through it all.

It is not only the cross but the resurrection of Jesus that gives hope in such events. By those two events the Church of God lives and dies.

Then and Now

The events of September 1991, although now a distant memory for many, have left their wounds. Some of their effects may never heal or, perhaps, scar tissue will remain a painful reminder.

This book started out with my own as yet uncompleted spiritual journey. I now wish to conclude with reflections which point into the unknown future. Like any signpost, they prominently display the destination even if the journey may be fraught with hazards, twists and turns.

The immediate effects of the tragedy - sleepless nights, tears, spending time with the bereaved, leading the church in worship in the atmosphere that surrounded the period of the accident – are all in the past. What is perceived of God in the here and now? Was He there on that Friday? Has He now retreated into heaven? Where is He?

Obviously the 'normal' demands of the ordained ministry take over, by way of church councils, evangelism in the shape of parish mission, baptisms, weddings and funerals, all high points in people's lives. Nevertheless, a tragic event like this leaves an indelible mark on one's life. 'Professional' as the ordained ministry should be, it can never be treated as a 'job'. Life is ministry – ministry is life, though it should not be without its times of real relaxation, hobbies and holidays.

I now would claim to have a greater understanding of the secular world in which the Church is set as a witness. For me it is a largely empty world, not devoid of meaning, yet, put simply, it is like time before creation, 'without shape or form' (Genesis 1:2). There is, as Quakers would claim, some light in all men and women but, in my judgement, it is all but extinguished by sin and selfishness. There may be attendance at rites of passage but for many, God can be forgotten for much of the time.

There is a need to highlight the absence of God in today's society. We live in a very different world from the one in the Bible when God seems to be involved. Our world is in the main dominated by materialistic values and the desire to survive. It is a world where the biblical understanding of 'love', for example, is perverted and abused. Certainly, it is not without hope as many have found to their joy (and cost). I have now learned to agonise more closely with those who are outside Christ's family and not to condemn, though that would be all too easy, but to feel their 'angst' and, at the same time, to rejoice in all God is doing and can do, both for them and for me.

Appendix A

Sample Questionnaire

This was submitted to each person interviewed, and their replies are recorded under appendices B, C and D.

There are few people who go through life without some form of crisis, but obviously some occupations have to face trauma in their professional duties far more than many other jobs. For example, although television programmes such as *London's Burning* and *Casualty* compare very differently with, say, the comfortable images of *Z Cars* or, further back, *Dixon of Dock Green* in their crisis management, they all show professional people in situations of real stress.

1. Can you remember where you were when the Akers Way accident occurred?
2. What was your response at the time?
3. What special training have you had for dealing with such traumatised situations?
4. What after-effects, e.g. post traumatic stress disorder, have you felt since?
   (a) Mentally?
   (b) Physically?
   (c) and Spiritually?
   How long did it/they last?
5. How were you able to relax and cope with such effects?
6. What back up and support systems exist for someone in your role? Do/ did they prove adequate?
7. What advice can you offer to others who may have to face similar situations?
8. In your opinion, is there any need for inter-disciplinary discussion and support amongst those who face such crises?

9.   Does age/sex/marital status/experience/authority have any
     bearing on the ability to cope?
10. Are there any special religious/moral insights that are
     helpful to be borne in mind in such situations?
11. Can you give three good examples and three bad examples
     of 'crisis' management?

Appendix B

Interview with
assistant hospital chaplain

1. I was off duty at home and received a brief telephone summons from the hospital chaplain at Princess Margaret Hospital to the effect that there had been a bad accident involving children and I was required at the Accident and Emergency Department of the hospital.

2. I immediately made the journey by car from Highworth to Princess Margaret Hospital which took about 17–20 minutes, where I met the chaplain in the accident area and was asked to go to the relatives' room in the Accident and Emergency Department.

3. I attended a lecture on post traumatic stress syndrome by a Wing Commander from Princess Alexandra Hospital, Wroughton, in respect of the Gulf War casualties, etc. Also my experience in Princess Margaret Hospital with Accident Unit admissions and maternity/infant deaths.

    I also attended a meeting in London after the Clapham/King's Cross incidents about responses to major incidents by chaplains and clergy.

4. (a) Mentally – I was pitched into a family grief situation with scant knowledge of what had occurred and the distressed mother and (twin sister) daughter with whom I was particularly involved were hardly able to put me in the picture. It was hard to know how to cope with the long silences and then outbursts of grief and vengeful sentiments.

    (b) Physically – I was in their company for about seven hours which was exhausting, and I was mindful of the fact

I was due to drive to Norwich the next day for a family wedding.

(c)   Spiritually – I often wonder if I did the right thing just to stay with them and facilitate their contact with the estranged father who was on holiday in Cornwall on a caravan site. This was managed eventually. I felt quite drained afterwards and got to bed at 4.00 a.m.

5.   I think it was a good thing I was committed to drive to Norwich at midday on the 14th. I had to concentrate on other things.

6.   I was able to talk to the hospital chaplain before going off duty and was able to tell my wife just the bare outline of what had happened and how I had been involved. The debriefing was helpful and I felt OK. There is a very good staff support scheme in existence for all employees of Swindon Health Authority.

7.   Arrange to talk to someone afterwards by way of debriefing before going off duty. Share at the time with others involved. Don't go it alone if at all possible.

8.   Yes. Perhaps through Hospital Staff Stress Syndrome Co-ordinator or Deanery Chapter, etc.

9.   All aspects leading to mature reflection or experience are useful. No one thing such as age on its own has bearing.

10.   I would make a distinction between spiritual needs and religious needs. Religious needs may have to be met later on. However, spiritual needs involving respect for life and property in respect of individuality, privacy and lifestyle, etc., respect of relationships and aspirations, all have to be brought into the attempt to meet spiritual needs as they arise at the time of an incident. It would rarely be an opportunity for direct reference to religious topics – unless they were raised by the individual involved. Then the field is open to give appropriate assurance of God's knowledge of every situation and his overall compassion for those caught up in humanly contrived incidents and disasters.

11.   I find it hard to think of examples but good ones would be: the motorway pile-up and fire on 13 February, 1991. The system of support debriefing for staff was very helpful. An emergency alert by way of practice shortly after helped

me to know what went wrong and the debriefing after that, even though it was not real, was very good. I would hope for another on the same lines before long. 'Bad' would have to be my own personal experience in divorce support. I went to another parish for a while but, apart from the offer of a few meals, there was no counselling or help from any ordained ministers either locally or from a diocesan level. I was just left to muddle through.

At the time of writing the original paper only one member of the hospital clergy team was available to answer the prepared questionnaire.

A further observation from the senior hospital chaplain

Just as people tend to remember what they were doing when President Kennedy was shot, when Prince Charles announced his engagement, etc., so I can remember, as if it were only yesterday, what I was doing when the major incidents occurred that have taken place during my thirteen years of ministry as hospital chaplain – the Hungerford shootings, the fireball on the M4, and a few incidents less well-known to the public, but equally traumatic. So it was with the Akers Way incident. I was attending a retirement party for a senior consultant in a hospital on the other side of Swindon when my bleep sounded. On answering the call I was informed by a sister in the Accident Unit that a terrible road accident had taken place in which several young people and children had been injured or killed. As I drove my car the four miles or so across the town, my mind was racing, as it always does at such a time. What would I find when I got there? What would I have to do? How many casualties and families would there be?

I have received training in working in very traumatic and stressful situations, critical incident debriefing and post traumatic stress. I believe that such training and previous experience provide an awareness, understanding and a professional stance which is necessary and important. It sustains me whilst I get on with 'thinking on my feet' and reacting from instinct as I try to respond appropriately to the patient, the parent, the friend, the relative, whom I find myself standing or sitting alongside.

Emotions are raw at those moments, guts are wrenched,

people spill out their anger, their desolation, despair, disbelief, guilt and so much else. What is my role? I try to be there to bring some containment into what, I guess, may feel like a world fallen apart. I attempt to accept and hold these emotions *as they are*. Not trying to change them, or to take them away, or to make them different. This is how it is and *it is awful*. I am standing in a small room with a family around a bed on which lies the dead body of their child, and I have no answers as to 'Why?' If I attempted to try, I believe it would be an insult. I am here to make it possible for them to vent their emotions and know that there is someone who can take it and to hold them whilst they do it.

It goes on into the night, one family after another. Afterwards, I need help. I am affected, as is every other member of staff and every person involved. In this Health Authority, now an NHS Trust, we have a Staff Support Service and a Psychology Service which offer support and critical incident stress debriefing. I also have my own professional supervisor whom I meet with weekly to assist me in reflecting upon my work. In 1991 I was also a member of a support group for hospital staff which gave me the space and emotionally held me whilst I allowed myself to be aware of my feelings about the incident and my part in it.

I am no longer a member of this group but in its place I am now in personal psychotherapy and this sustains me in a similar way. These means of support are vital for me if I am to be able to continue in this sort of work. I cannot properly offer support to others if I am not held and supported myself.

I hope that what may be learned from such a terrible event is that *everyone* whose work makes these kind of physical, spiritual and emotional demands upon them, also have their own needs. This is true for medical staff, nurses, members of the emergency services, social workers, *and clergy*. Opportunities to 'de-brief' and have these needs recognised and heard should be made available, not only in the event of a major tragedy, but on a regular basis. It doesn't matter how old, how experienced, what family we have, or even if we have a faith in a God who we believe does love us despite what we see happening around us – we are all human beings. These situations reach into the depths of our beings and hook into our own experiences and personal history. None of us are immune from the pain of human suffering.

Appendix C

Interview with police inspector

1. I was on the motorway dealing with a young mother and children who had broken down and were reported to be walking along the central reservation.

2. I received a call from the control room sergeant saying there had been a serious accident which I should attend and I knew that, if he said I should attend, it was very serious and the intonation in his voice indicated it was no ordinary accident.

3. We do not actually run courses for dealing with such incidents but through our probation we are tutored by a senior police constable. In the early stages you would perhaps have to go and break the news of a death from a road traffic accident accompanied by that officer, ensuring the situation was dealt with causing as little trauma as possible to the family. We now have 'peer counsellors' which is new for the 1990s; you have to feel you can trust them but if you are in a stressful situation you can now go and talk, and they can help you. There is also a Force Welfare Officer who is able to put you in touch with someone professional to help you through your stressful time if you really are badly affected. Confidentiality is very important.

4. (a) The first three days were particularly difficult because on top of the trauma of what I had witnessed at the scene, I had the added pressure of being the officer investigating the accident and ensuring it was all dealt with professionally. I also had to cope with the multitude of press and media interviews.

   (b) Physically it was difficult to sleep. I was overtired

and the brain kept going over and over the enquiries that had to be done – had I done this or that? One of the difficulties which didn't help was that one of the accused was in hospital and we were unable to speak to him. It was very traumatic at the hospital on the night and I saw several nurses in tears. Why I don't know, but I can remember thinking to myself, 'If I can cope, why can't you?'

(c) I think at that time the only concern I had was for the traffic officers dealing with it and that they should be OK. I was very mindful that some were young and not used to any incident of this kind and making sure they had the courage to say if they could not cope. In such an incident you go into neutral and deal with the situation, the body turns off and you just do the job you are paid to do. When a nasty incident has to be dealt with you do not think how terrible, how awful, it is just a case of getting on and sorting out the job. You reflect on it all after in the quiet moments.

5. Always talk to someone about it. This applies to all stress-ful situations, don't bottle it up. In our job unfortunately, it soon becomes just another job and the next tragedy takes its place. You are always mindful that the public need you as their prop and your own welfare takes second place. Don't ever think we wouldn't like to cry along with them at times. It was very difficult with the religious beliefs of some of the relatives to say the right thing for comfort. It is nice to be able to say they have all gone to heaven together, but, if they do not believe in God then these words are meaningless. This is the first occasion when we have had such in-depth and lengthy involvement with relatives.

6. No one asked me if I was all right or the officers on traffic. We were expected to cope.

7. It is very hard to offer advice. You have to admit you are human, be able to seek out someone and admit you are not infallible. It helps to talk to a colleague who can understand what you are going through. You have to find your own way of coping with problems. Different incidents affect you in different ways.

8. The families were offered the services of Cruse, but did

not take up the offer. It's very difficult in the first week on any big incident to find enough time to sit down with other agencies and discuss the incident. I didn't feel they appreciated the vast amount of work the police have to do. I found it easier to relate to you because I felt you were there as an independent counsellor, knew how to support when necessary and what was required and I could get on with the job I had to do. I felt we were on the same wavelength. I don't decry the other agencies and the help they give, but I think once they've offered help and it's been refused, then the relatives should be allowed to get the support from wherever they wish.

9. Working as I do in a very male-dominated organisation I find I cope with incidents sometimes better than the men and don't have to pretend like they do to support the macho image. Women are more susceptible to the grieving side and I can be more outwardly affected by a cot death. We exchange roles with the other two emergency services to get a better appreciation of each other's jobs. I spent time with the Ambulance Service and the last job of the day was to help a man in considerable pain dying from cancer into an ambulance. He was taken to the hospice and I was aware it was his last journey and he'd never return home again. It upset me for days and I never want a task like that again. Yet I can go to an accident where someone is dying or dead and it does not have the same effect.

10. I always say it is no good calling yourself a Christian if you do not have faith. I was brought up in a religious family to go to Church, etc. I do believe all those children have gone to heaven and are all there together, wherever you believe 'heaven' to be, and that gives me comfort that they are all being looked after. I do have that faith. When things get really, really bad, and they sometimes do in the police force, it is only my inbuilt faith which gets me through. People are important and you have to be able to talk to them in a way they can understand. It is important to relate to people.

11. Probably this has been covered already, but at times we have an inability within management itself to appreciate people are going through a bad time and not do something

about it. I thought it ironic that the fire brigade, whose involvement that night was the least, had their chaplain waiting for them on their return to the station. There was no one waiting for any of the police officers; but then again, society always expected us just to get on with it.

Appendix D

Interview with social services manager

I am Child Care Manager with the Social Services.

1. No, I cannot remember.
2. Surprise and sympathy for the families involved.
3. Within general social work training we are normally given some fundamental training on bereavement counselling and, because of special interest, over the years, in various jobs I have held I have tried to develop that but, in crisis situations, no special training.
4. I had no dealing with the families so it does not really apply to me.
5. This does not apply.
6. Apart from normal reporting very little at my level; but for social workers involved there is a policy initiative which states that where workers are involved in any trauma, e.g. any serious abuse case, the department does agree to private neutral counselling support.
7. & 8. In terms of disasters of great magnitude, I feel there is a need for agencies to have an awareness of the effect it will have on their work. I feel, because of some work I was doing arising out of the Gulf conflict, there is a need at an early stage to know and understand the roles of everyone likely to be involved so that duplication does not take place.
9. Yes. I think nothing can truly prepare you for something such as a disaster which has a personal effect on you or your family but I do feel children, generally in society, are less able to cope because on the whole they are not communicated with in a proper sense. The thought of discussing things which are personal is so daunting,

and children are often objects of pity. I feel children are particularly disadvantaged and traumatised by an invasion into what they see as a secure world. Most of us, by the time we reach adult life, have experienced certain situations which help us, but children do not have such experience to help them.

10. I personally find no comforting religious insight into coping with grief and what seems clearly unjust in that situation, although because I can see no logic or pattern to it does not diminish my own personal belief in God, but it does make me view the universe as a stark and inhospitable place.

11. Speaking from my own experience, vis-a-vis the Gulf crisis when people had time to prepare themselves for what seemed to be a challenging period, it may be easier to start with bad examples. I felt that when senior management come together they often feel the need to put their own stamp on how things should be managed and the effect is that it can actually often restrict and confine people at lower levels and inhibit communication.

There is an intense well-meaning desire to get it right but it does not actually prove helpful. Bad again: insularity in that one organisation or group feels they have a dominant share in the work to be done without considering what others can give to the situation. Good: regular meetings to allow support and sharing of resources, and breaking down into smaller support group networks. Prior to the Gulf crisis we had not got to that stage and we were previously very much regimented.

Notes

1. Michael Ramsey, *The Christian Priest Today*, SPCK, 1985.
2. George Carey, *The Gate of Glory*, Hodder, 1986.
3. Alan Billings, 'Keeping Chaos at Bay', Church of England Board of Social Responsibility Journal *Together*, January 1990.
4. John Harris, *Stress, Power and Ministry*, Alban Institute, 1977.
5. Peter Rudge, *Management and Ministry*, McGraw Hill, 1976.
6. *Parson Woodforde Diaries 1759–1802*, Tiger Books International, 1991.
7. J.M. Shields CF, 'Lockerbie Disaster', *Royal Army Chaplains' Journal*, January 1990.
8. Frank Parkinson, *Royal Army Chaplains' Journal*, July 1989.
9. Stuart Turner, *Psychiatry Today*, August 1992.
10. Sheila Cassidy, *Sharing the Darkness*, Darton, Longman and Todd, 1988.
11. Stephen Homewood, *Zeebrugge 'A Hero's Story'*, Bloomsbury Press, 1989.
    (Further reading on this subject relating to Chapter 6 may be found in *The Concise Oxford Textbook of Psychiatry* and *Post Trauma Stress* by Frank Parkinson.)
12. Keith Ward, quoted by David Cockerell in the *Crucible*, January/March 1990.
13. F. Jurgen Moltmann, *Experiences of God*, SCM, 1980.
14. F. Jurgen Moltmann, *The Crucified God*, SCM, 1974.
15. Sheila Cassidy, *Good Friday People*, Darton, Longman and Todd, 1991.

16. John Hick, *Evil and the God of Love*, SCM, 1968.
17. Charles Colson, *Who Speaks for God*? Hodder, 1988.
18. Quoted by Alan Wilkinson in *The Church of England and the First World War*, SPCK, 1978.
19. J.B. Philips, *Your God is Too Small*, Epworth Press, 1956.
20. Erik Peterson, *The Search for Unity in a Dynamic Religion*, Westview Press, 1988.
21. Charles Ohlrich, *The Suffering God*, Triangle Press, 1982.
22. Air Vice-Marshal David Brook – 'Dealing with Disaster', quoted in *The Daily Telegraph*, August 1992.
23. Most of the references here are drawn from material supplied by the Church of England Communications Unit in their submissions (1992) (i) to Mr Clive Soley MP in his Private Member's bill (Freedom and Responsibility of the Press); (ii) The National Heritage Committee enquiry into privacy and media intrusion; (iii) the Calcutt review of self-regulation by the press.
24. *Victims Twice Over*, National Association of Victim Support Schemes, 1992.
25. Louise Patten, article in the *Daily Telegraph*, September 1994.
26. Anthony Russell, *The Clerical Profession*, SPCK, 1980.
27. Alan Billings, op. cit.
28. Roger Grainger, *The Meaning of the Rite*, Lutterworth Press, 1985.
29. Elaine Ramshaw, *Ritual and Pastoral Care*, Fortress Press, 1987.
30. Iona and Peter Opie, *The Lore and Language of School Children*, Oxford University Press, 1959.
31. C.S. Lewis, *A Grief Observed*, Faber, 1966.

For further reading see also *The World's Greatest Disasters*, Joyce Robins, Hamlyn, 1990.